The Bolinas-Fairfax Road

The History of One of Marin's Most Scenic Roads

By Brian K. Crawford

BOLINAS ROAD NEAR SAN RAFAEL

The Crawford Press
San Anselmo, California

Contents

Introduction

View of Bolinas from Bolinas Ridge

The Bolinas-Fairfax Road in central Marin County, just north of San Francisco, is unquestionably one of the most beautiful roads in the country. Sometimes known to locals as the Bofax, it is notoriously narrow, steep, and twisting. The two-lane blacktop drive winds through dense redwood forests, traces the shores of a sparkling mountain lake, crosses a high narrow dam, climbs two precipitous ridges, and at the summit of the Bolinas Ridge provides a heart-stopping view of Point Reyes, the wide sweep of the Pacific Ocean, and Bolinas Lagoon more than 1500 feet below. Hundreds of car commercials have been filmed on the road's scenic curves. The Bolinas-Fairfax also provides access to scores of popular hiking and mountain biking trails and fishing spots on several beautiful mountain lakes, as well as a less-crowded route to Mount Tamalpais than the road from Mill Valley. Bicyclists love the challenges of the long grinding climbs and exhilarating downhill runs.

1

Though it's less than twenty miles long, it has over three hundred turns, some so tight even a compact car has trouble staying in the lane. This makes every drive an adventure, especially at night or in the frequent fogs. During winter storms, landslides and fallen trees frequently close the road, sometimes for months. Imagine what it was like more than a hundred years ago, when you would have made the trip by stagecoach on an unpaved dirt road.

Bolinas-Fairfax Road along Alpine Lake

I first discovered the road when my wife and I moved to Marin in 1986. I set out to explore the many trails along the road—Azalea Hill, Blue Ridge, Pine Mountain, Little Carson Falls, the Cataracts, and so many more.

There was a severe drought at the time, and the reservoirs were very low. One day while hiking along the exposed bottom of Alpine Lake, I discovered the foundations of a number of buildings, well below the normal water line. Curious, I began delving into local history and discovered that they were the remains of Liberty Ranch, a resort on the old San Rafael to Bolinas Stagecoach road. Since there is no such road today, stagecoaches or not, curiosity led me to research the old road. I

2

traced the original route and scoured the newspapers and library references to learn the history of the road and the people who built and used it.

Fascinating stories began turning up of the pioneers and eccentric characters who built the road, the families that lived along it, and of stagecoach accidents, holdups, brush fires, and haunted jail cells. The story became entwined with that of the Marin Municipal Water District and their various dams, and with other connecting roads—the Eldridge, Fairfax, Shaver, Fish, and Makin grades.

After almost thirty years of research, I had amassed a considerable amount of material that is not generally known and to my knowledge has never been gathered together. These stories begged to be told, but they were scattered in time and subject matter. The common thread was the road that started it all, the Bolinas-Fairfax. I concentrated my research on learning all I could about the road, talking with historians, reading everything I could find, and scanning old newspapers. I volunteered at the County Library's Schroeder Maps Collection, studying and cataloging the original field notebooks and hand-drawn maps of the men who surveyed and built the road. This book is the result.

Although most Marinites are familiar with the Bolinas-Fairfax, few know about its rich history, of how it was built, and why. Many would be surprised to learn that it did not start out as a road between Bolinas and Fairfax at all. It has had additions and subtractions and changed its route many times since it was first built. This is the story of this beloved road and how it came to be.

ACKNOWLEDGEMENTS

The book would not exist were it not for the kindness and assistance of many people. These include Dewey Livingston of the Jack Mason Museum of West Marin History in Inverness; Laurie Thompson, Librarian of the Anne T. Kent California Room at the Marin County Free Library; Elia Haworth, Curator of the Bolinas Museum; Bill Schroeder, who sold his immense collection of historic maps to the County; Judy Coy of the San Anselmo Historical Museum; Fran Cappelletti of the José Moya del Piño Library in Ross; Matt Cerkel of the Marin Municipal Water District; and local historians Brad Rippe, Brian Sagar, Fred Runner, Tim Wood, Nick Fain, Joe Breeze, Nancy Skinner, and many others. I am grateful to them all.

The Petition, 1877

Marin County is a peninsula bounded on the west by the Pacific, on the east by San Pablo Bay and San Francisco Bay, and on the south by the Golden Gate. The southern half of the county, though within a long walk of San Francisco, is still largely undeveloped open space, isolated by steep ridges and the almost 2,600-foot Mount Tamalpais. US-101 runs up the eastern shore from the Golden Gate Bridge through the population centers of Sausalito, Mill Valley, Corte Madera, San Rafael, and Novato. But the streaming lines of commuters and tourists rushing north and south see little of the real county. Most of the southern and western parts of the county, consisting of steep grassy or tree-clad ridges, steep ravines, and dense stands of redwoods, is protected from development. 290 square miles, 56% of the land area of the county, is permanently protected. The Golden Gate National Recreation Area, Muir Woods National Monument, Point Reyes National Seashore, Mount Tamalpais State Park, Samuel P. Taylor State Park, twenty-one county parks, thirty-four county open space preserves, scores of local parks, ranches protected by the Marin Agricultural Land Trust, and the vast watershed of the Marin Municipal Water District guarantee that this land will be protected forever.

Few roads cross this huge expanse. Sir Francis Drake Boulevard runs from Point San Quentin, almost the easternmost point in the county, forty miles to Point Reyes Lighthouse, the westernmost tip, bisecting the county. CA-1, the famous Shoreline Highway, clings to the precipitous cliffs along the west coast. But for much of its history, there was no direct route between the county seat at San Rafael and the seaside town of Bolinas.

Bolinas, now a small town, was a much busier place a hundred and fifty years ago. In the 1850s, two-thirds of Marin's residents lived in Bolinas Township. A thriving lumber industry cut the massive coastal redwoods. Sawmills processed the logs for the buildings and wharves of San Francisco. Copper mines and lime kilns dotted the steep canyons. Bolinas Lagoon had not yet silted in, and schooners sailed in to take away the lumber and ore. Several shipyards operated there and built more than a dozen schooners. Ranching, dairy farms, and commercial fishing and crabbing provided produce. Residents of San Rafael and San Francisco liked to get away to Bolinas on weekends to picnic, swim, fish, hunt, and hike. Bolinas was also a popular destination for longer vacations, with two large waterfront hotels and an extensive resort of tent cabins nearby called Willow Camp (now Stinson Beach).

But for many years it was hard to get to Bolinas at all. The fastest way was to take a schooner from San Francisco or Sausalito to the Bolinas embarcadero inside the lagoon. But it was pricey and the trip was not without risk. Many of these schooners ran aground and were lost, either on the rocky, foggy coast of southern Marin, or on Duxbury Reef, stretching nearly across the mouth of the lagoon.

The only alternative to the schooners was to walk or ride a horse twenty miles from San Rafael over Mount Tamalpais on the old trail built by the Miwok Indians, a challenging physical exertion, and unsuitable for wagons.

In 1865 a dirt road was built from San Rafael west twenty miles to Olema, called the Olema Road or sometimes just the County Road—now Sir Francis Drake Boulevard. It followed an earlier Indian trail later used by the Mexican families who settled Bolinas in 1837. For many years this route was the only connection between the more developed eastern section of the county and the remote and rural western section.

In 1868 a road was built running twelve miles south from Olema to Bolinas. It was now possible to drive a wagon or carriage from San Rafael to Bolinas, but it was a thirty-mile drive—an exhausting ten-hour ride. For Bolinas residents, even a casual visit to family or a doctor's appointment meant two days of travel and an overnight stay.

Bolinas was much closer to Sausalito, but building a road between these two towns proved very challenging. The heights of Mount Tamalpais plunge directly into the sea along a dramatic iron-bound coastline. In 1870 a road was blasted into the cliffs from Sausalito to Willow Camp, but Bolinas Lagoon, larger and deeper then, ran right up against the vertical cliffs, preventing the road from reaching Bolinas.

If the tide were very low, a daring driver could take a wagon across the mudflats under the beetling cliffs, but the normal procedure was for the stages to unload passengers and freight at McKennan's Landing, two miles beyond Willow Camp, where they signaled for Bill McKennan in Bolinas to come pick them up in his gasoline launch, the *Alice F.*

Bolinas area showing the route of the Olema-Bolinas stage from the north and the Sausalito-Willow Camp stage from the south.

6

A third alternative was to take the Sausalito stage to Willow Camp, walk three miles along the sand spit to the Bolinas Channel, then shout for a pickup. "Chicken Charley" Burgeson would often come over in a rowboat to pick up passengers for a small fee.

In 1875 the North Pacific Coast Railroad was completed. It was a narrow-gauge line that ran from Sausalito through Fairfax to Tomales Bay at Point Reyes Station, then north along the bay to Cazadero in Sonoma County. A spur connected to San Rafael. This new line opened up the western portions of the county considerably. Farmers, fishermen, and loggers could haul their products to Point Reyes Station instead of all the way to San Rafael, saving a day's drive. Yet Bolinas, which had lobbied for the railroad, had been bypassed. The nearest station was at Point Reyes Station, fourteen miles away.

The train revolutionized recreation as well. Visitors from San Francisco could take the ferries to either Sausalito or Point San Quentin, then the train to Point Reyes Station, and finally the stagecoach for the fourteen miles south to Bolinas, but it was still a long all-day trip.

The logging and mining operations around Bolinas stripped the slopes of their ancient trees, increasing sediment flow into Bolinas Lagoon. Combined with the normal flow of sand along the beach, this caused the entrance to become shallower and narrower, and the larger schooners could no longer get into the bay. The logging, mining, and shipbuilding industries declined disastrously. With fewer lumber schooners plying between the bay and San Francisco, the opportunities for passengers and freight declined as well. People from San Francisco and San Rafael wanted an easier way to get to Bolinas, and Bolinas residents wanted to get their goods to market more quickly, but the shoreline town was more isolated than ever. A shorter way was clearly needed.

A group of prominent citizens called a meeting and drafted a petition to the Board of Supervisors, requesting the construction of a more direct road between San Rafael and Bolinas. They decided the best route would be to build the road from Bolinas to Fairfax, where it would connect with both the railroad and the San Rafael-Olema Road. They presented their petition at the Board meeting on Monday, February 5, 1877:

To the Hon. Board of Supervisors of Marin County:
    We, the undersigned, your petitioners, inhabitants of Road Districts Nos. 3 and 6, in Marin County, would most

respectfully represent to your honorable Board the necessity of the laying out and construction of a public road in said Road Districts, over and along the following described route, viz: Beginning at the point about 150 yards easterly from Bresson's saloon[1], near the Fairfax Picnic Grounds, at which the road to said saloon and picnic grounds leaves the San Rafael and Olema road, said place of beginning being about 3½ miles westerly from the town of San Rafael. Running thence southwesterly and westerly along and in the vicinity of the old San Rafael and Bolinas trail to the easterly ascent of the Bolinas Ridge. Thence over said ridge by the most practicable route to the Bay of Bolinas, connecting with the county road which runs along the northeasterly shore of said Bay at the point known as the mouth of Little Greenwood Gulch[2]. The above described route passes over the lands of Mrs. M. M. Sais[3], of Saunders, McRea [McRae] and Bush, of the estate of Jas. Ross. Sr., of Messrs. Shafter & Howard, of Samuel Weeks and of Peter Bourn[e]. Your petitioners are not informed as to whether the owners of the lands over which the above described route passes will consent to the laying out of the road hereby petitioned for, or what will be the probable cost for the right of way for the same. Your petitioners would ask the early attention of your honorable Board to the subject matter of this petition—

First—For the reason that the present means of communication between the fertile and populous region known as Bolinas and the county seat is only by traveling over a distance more than twice as far it would be by the route petitioned for; the distance between San Rafael and Bolinas Bay being less than 7½ miles in a straight line, and by the road hereby petitioned for would not exceed 10 miles, whereas, by any public road now traveled the distance is more than 20 miles.

Second—The laying out and construction of the road petitioned for will, in the opinion of your petitioners, add materially to the lands over and along which it passes.

---

[1] Operated by Paul Bresson near the corner of Bolinas and Broadway in Fairfax.
[2] Named for John Greenwood (1827-?), son of famed pathfinder and wagon train guide Caleb Greenwood (1763-1850). The canyon was later named Thompson Gulch, and is now Garden Club Canyon in Audubon Canyon Ranch.
[3] Maria Manuela Miranda Sais (1814-1891), widow of Domingo Sais (1806-1853), first non-Indian settler in San Anselmo.

Third —It will open up for the public travel one of the most attractive sections of country in the county, and which is now almost inaccessible by ordinary means of conveyance.

Your petitioners therefore pray that your honorable Board will take such action as shall be for the public benefit, and in accordance with law. (Signed) Henry H. Bigelow, Albert Dibblee, P. K. Austin, T. G. Gray, W. W. Wilkins, Jas. H. Morse Jr., Wells Case, B. G. Morse, A. D. Easkoot, H. B. Mills, S. McCurdy, C. M. Howard, Estate of O. L. Shafter, W. Evans, Samuel Clark, Robt. Ingram, Jas. D. Walker.

Marin County Journal, 8 February 1877

The petitioners were major landowners and influential men. Dibblee owned much of Ross; Shafter and Howard owned all of Point Reyes and much of the county besides; Easkoot was a civil engineer and former county surveyor. The Morses, McCurdy, Wilkins and Ingram were prominent ranchers in Bolinas. The Board of Supervisors listened to them:

The Board ordered a preliminary survey of the route above laid out and [to produce a] report, a plat, profile, and field notes, with an estimate of the cost-expense not to exceed $70.

Marin County Journal, 8 February 1877

The first hurdle was cleared toward the construction of the road. But where exactly would the road run? The Board of Supervisors considered changing the eastern terminus of the road from Fairfax to San Rafael. No doubt they thought the stage line would be good for business in San Rafael, a much bigger town than Fairfax. And much of the travel from Bolinas was to do business at the new Greek revival County Courthouse, built just five years earlier.

To determine the best route for the new road, the supervisors turned to the County Surveyor, "Professor" Hiram Austin.

9

Map by Gary D. Crawford

The Surveyor

Hiram Spellman Austin is largely forgotten today, but he left a lasting mark on Marin. Many of our most famous and beautiful country roads were designed by him, including portions of the Shoreline Highway, Sir Francis Drake Boulevard, Lucas Valley Road, the Eldridge Grade, and of course the Bolinas-Fairfax.

He also laid out railroads, sewers and water lines, established the boundaries of hundreds of ranches and other properties, laid out subdivisions, and in 1873 created the first accurate and definitive map of all of Marin County.

Austin also began a collection of survey maps of the county which was passed down through generations of surveyors, each adding to it, until it contains many thousands of historical maps, field notebooks, job orders and invoices, and correspondence from over a century and a half of surveying in Marin. This collection was acquired by the Marin County Free Library and is currently being cataloged and conserved.

In J. P. Munro-Fraser's 1880 *History of Marin County California*, we find the well-traveled Austin's biography:

Hiram Austin was born in Portage County, Ohio, November 27, 1820, and there resided, attended school and worked on his father's farm for the first few years of his life; teaching school for a time when but seventeen. His taste running in the direction of mechanical studies, at the age of twenty he commenced surveying. In 1852 he left Portage for Park County, Indiana, and here began the dairying and cheese making business, combining therewith some engineering and surveying. He resided there for four years, when he moved to Columbia County, Wisconsin, where he opened a prairie farm and resided until 1859, when he moved to Macoupin County, Illinois, and there embarked in farming and surveying. In December, 1861, he came to California via Panama, and at once took up a residence in

Marin County. He engaged in farming in Bolinas for three years, when, in 1864, he was elected to be County Surveyor on the Republican ticket. In 1865 he moved his residence to San Rafael. Mr. Austin has been County Surveyor until the election of 1879, and during his terms of office has done much valuable service, among others the completion of a very correct and handsome county map.

In spite of his prominence and his accomplishments, Austin is a rather mysterious figure. His name appears in Marin newspapers frequently between 1867 and 1887 in connection with his various projects, but other than that, there's no mention of the man attending an event, joining a group, or traveling. The 1870 and 1880 census records show him living in a hotel on Fourth Street in San Rafael. In 1870 he was single; in 1880, married, though not living with his wife. There is no record of his family, social interactions, or indeed his life. In over a quarter century of residence in Marin, the only personal note in the papers is this:

Severely Injured.—On Tuesday last Hiram Austin, Esq., County Surveyor, was seriously injured by being thrown from a buggy while on his way from the Reed Ranch to San Rafael. At present writing however, he is getting along well.

Marin County Journal, 17 April 1869.

Around 1887, after fourteen years as Marin County Surveyor, he moved to Placerville and was appointed county surveyor in El Dorado County. He died there in April 1893, aged seventy-two. The *Marin County Tocsin*, a sometimes sensationalist newspaper operated by James H. Wilkins in San Rafael, published this remarkable obituary of Austin:

The news comes to the *Tocsin* office of the death of Hiram Austin, at Placerville, El Dorado County, where he moved after leaving San Rafael seven or eight years ago. The old gentleman had continued the practice of the profession of civil engineering there, had been elected County Surveyor and we believe his circumstances of late years have been fairly comfortable.

The deceased was one of the most noted characters around Marin County in the early days. He was universally known as the "Professor," partly because he had never been one and partly perhaps for the same reasons that induce some people to apply that title to the editor of this paper. From way back in the early fifties[4] down to the time when he left this section, he held the office of County Surveyor with only one or two breaks in the succession. He either conducted or was connected with about all the important surveys upon which much of the titles to property rights in Marin depend and it is safe to say that he made acquaintance in a professional way with every acre in the county.

How the old man managed to get through the vast tramps, often over high mountain ranges and the roughest kind of country, which his occupation demanded, was a mystery. His bulk was enormous and anyone who looked at his aldermanic proportions, would have considered that he was doing well if he managed to walk around a level block without a stroke of apoplexy and this impression was strengthened by the fact that on the slightest exertion he blew and wheezed worse than a spermaceti whale. Yet, notwithstanding these apparent handicaps, he got there just the same and usually a little better than the athletic young men who prided themselves on their physical powers. Occasionally some of his field men, not posted on the facts, engaged in conspiracies to rush work over a rough piece of country and break the "Professor" down. The intended victim was always on the lookout for schemes of the sort and the upshot of them was invariably that the conspirators found themselves imploring the old man, in the name of everything beautiful and sacred, to give them a rest.

In the early days, when work was abundant and the compensation of Surveyors about anything they chose to ask, Austin must have made a bucketful of money every year. It did him no good, however. He had contracted the lavish habits that characterized young California and when he had money in his pocket his greatest concern seemed to be to find the easiest and most expeditious way of getting rid of it. A large circle of amiable acquaintances stood always ready to help him out in this line and between all hands they made such a success of it that even in the heyday of his fortunes, when he was in receipt of a

---

[4] This is inaccurate. Austin first came to California in 1861 and didn't become county surveyor until 1863.

princely revenue, he was constantly pursued by a horde of creditors, lived in a hovel, cooked for himself and was suspected of doing his own washing.   His utter recklessness in business matters and some other shortcomings often exasperated those who had dealings with him and by many he was harshly judged. Even in the solemn presence of death and writing with the charity that should be extended to the acts of those who can never reply to human criticism, it cannot be pretended that his life was all that it should have been. But on the other hand, it is true that he was a kind-hearted man, with many amiable qualities, and in most matters had a more correct standard than many whose weaknesses never led them into the follies that blighted Austin's career.

After he had lived in San Rafael for some years, it was discovered that he had made for himself a little private history before he came to the Pacific Coast. His true name was found to be Erastus Spellman. He had married early in life, but the attempt had proved a failure and a separation had followed. When he drifted westward, for some reason he sought to sink his old identity and assumed the name of Hiram Austin, which he clung to till the end notwithstanding the fact that everyone knew his true name. Singularly enough the pair who had found the married state insupportable in the spring-time of life, were reunited when the frosts and snows of their December had bleached the hair and furrowed the cheeks of the aged couple. Old Mrs. Austin (or Spellman) came to San Rafael to join her venerable husband about two years before he left for Placerville.   The union during their declining years seemed very happy, time probably having taught them the valuable lesson of mutual forbearance. They lived together till the end of the old Surveyor came a few days ago.

Marin County Tocsin, 29 April 1893

We can only wonder what Wilkins considered Austin's "lavish habits," "utter recklessness," "follies," and "other shortcomings." The story of his assumed name is also curious. If "everyone knew his true name," why bother with a pseudonym?

In fact, his wife (who is nowhere named) objected to the obituary, for two weeks later, on May 13, the *Tocsin* printed the following non-retraction:

A short time ago the *Tocsin* noted the death of ex-County Surveyor Hiram Austin and made somewhat extended mention of the deceased. The article was certainly not written in an unfriendly spirit. We had none but kind recollections of the old gentleman and had no desire to stir up a different feeling in others. The widow of the deceased has, however, taken deep exception and writes a bitter letter of complaint to this office. Among other things that she specially demurs to is the mention of the circumstance of his assuming the name of Hiram Austin, his veritable title being Festus Spellman. Every old time resident of the county believed this to be the fact, although we do not know upon what evidence. Mrs. Austin states that there is no foundation for the story. That her husband's true name was Hiram Spellman Austin and nothing else. We gladly give space to her version of it.

Wilkins didn't print the widow's letter and published only these few words for "her version of it," as he sniffed. For some reason he gave no credence to the idea that she might know her husband's name. And Wilkins calls Austin Erastus in the first article and Festus in the second. These are mysteries about Austin (or maybe Wilkins) that may never be resolved.

Whatever the truth about the man's character, Professor Austin was a professional and knew his work. At the beginning of May 1877 he and a small crew set out to do a preliminary survey to select a route for the new road from San Rafael to Bolinas. They were to report their results at the next meeting of the Board of Supervisors, only a month away.

The Route

US Coast Survey map of central Marin in 1873, surveyed by C. F. Hoffman. Table Mt. is the old name for Tamalpais, here applied to West Peak. Sugarloaf Hill is Red Hill in San Anselmo. Baulinas and Baulines are older spellings of Bolinas.

At the time of the gold rush, the population of the entire county was only 321. San Rafael was just a half-dozen houses clustered around the crumbling ruins of Mission San Rafael, which had been abandoned fifteen years before. San Rafael Creek was much larger then, a navigable estuary that extended all the way to Third and A Streets, with a turning basin and docks for the schooners to Petaluma and San Francisco. Wetlands covered the low areas along the creek. The old mission spring on San Rafael Hill continued to be the only water supply to the town.

In 1857 Scotsman James Ross (1812-1862) bought the Rancho Punta de San Quentin, almost fourteen square miles of rich land. South of town, where Corte Madera Creek flowed into the bay (roughly at the

College of Marin today), he built a number of warehouses, stores, and docks, and established a regular steamer service to carry the lumber and produce of the fertile valley to market in San Francisco. The small town of Ross Landing (now Kentfield), grew up around this landing. The valley came to be called Ross Valley.

Now twenty-five years later, the population of the county had soared to ten thousand. San Rafael had grown to more than fifteen hundred residents and was the county seat. The estuary had been filled in and rows of commercial buildings lined the new streets. The old buildings of Mission San Rafael had long ago fallen down and their materials had been reused. Only the mission's pear orchard remained[5]. The valley around the town was dotted with widely-spaced homes and small ranches. Orchards and vegetable gardens filled undeveloped lots. James McCue had built a reservoir on a hill southwest of San Rafael (still called Reservoir Hill, though the reservoir itself is long gone) and citizens enjoyed access to water and sewers and gas, two newspapers, two doctors and two railroads.

In 1871 the San Quentin and San Rafael Railroad was built running just three miles from southern San Rafael to the prison at San Quentin, terminating at the ferry docks built on a rock called Agnes Island (now within the foundations of the Richmond-San Rafael Bridge). The North Pacific Coast Railroad was still under construction from Sausalito out to the Pacific coast and up to Sonoma County. But because the 450-foot-high Southern Heights Ridge blocked access to San Rafael from the south, the NPCRR had been built up the Ross Valley, isolating San Rafael. In 1874 a spur line was added running east through the redwood-filled valley (now the Miracle Mile) to San Rafael. The railroad junction was called at first simply Junction, later renamed San Anselmo. Midway between Junction and Ross Landing, the small settlement of Ross had grown up around the NPCRR's new Sunnyside station.

The land Austin had to cross was rough and roadless, but hardly unexplored. Hiking, fishing, and hunting were popular sports, and many Marin residents had been up Mount Tamalpais for picnics and the spectacular views. Men and boys fanned out across the hills with their guns every August when deer season opened. There were dairy farms

---

[5] The last remaining scion of these trees is in the Marin Art and Garden Center in Ross.

and logging camps in a number of the valleys, with wagon tracks from the nearest town. Hunting and fishing cabins dotted the shady banks of Lagunitas Creek. So it was not entirely wilderness they were crossing. But for the most part, the route lay through thick forest and steep ridges, where only ancient Indian trails and deer trails gave access to the more remote parts of the county.

The central portion of this area was the valley of Lagunitas Creek, named for two small lakes[6]. The creek drained the north side of Mount Tamalpais, one of the rainiest regions of Marin. Its watershed was limited on the south by the three-mile-long east-west ridge of Tamalpais, more than two thousand feet high. At Rock Spring, the ridge made a sharp right-angle turn and ran eight miles northwest to Olema, forming the Bolinas Ridge. At fifteen hundred feet high, Bolinas Ridge would be a formidable obstacle for the road. Lagunitas Creek wound through this valley, roughly paralleling Bolinas Ridge, until it found its way around the northern end of the ridge near Point Reyes Station, where it emptied into Tomales Bay.

On the eastern side, the watershed was delimited by a much lower eight hundred-foot ridge separating it from the watershed of the Ross Valley. This too would have to be surmounted.

The Preliminary Survey

Austin recognized that there were only two practical gateways to this vast backcountry. The first was to branch off from the San Rafael-Olema Road at Fairfax and follow the route of the old San Rafael-Bolinas Trail

---

[6] One is the small lagoon now at the southeast corner of the Meadow Club. The other may have been Lily Lake.

into Lagunitas Valley. This was the route requested in the petition. The second was to follow Isaac Shaver's old logging track from the settlement of Ross. To allow the Board of Supervisors to choose between them, he would have to survey both. He started with Ross.

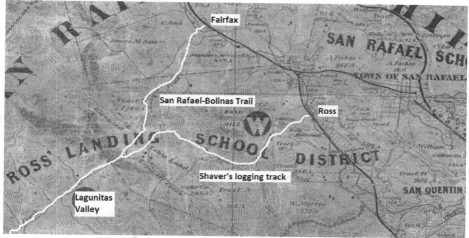

On Hiram Austin's 1873 map of Marin.

Ross Creek tumbled down from the high country, cutting a steep-walled canyon through a ridge of hills before emptying into Corte Madera Creek at Ross. Several woodchoppers had built cabins in Bill Williams Gulch just above, and they had created a rough track called Wood Road for dragging logs down this canyon to Ross.

In 1865 Isaac Shaver built a sawmill several miles farther up into the back country and built another logging road to his saw mill. In places the canyon was so narrow and steep that the wagons simply drove in the creek bed to haul the lumber to Shaver's dock at Ross Landing. Rough as it was, Austin decided to make use of the track wherever he could.

But to get from San Rafael to Ross, Austin faced the same problem the railroad had—Southern Heights Ridge. More than three miles long and in places more than four hundred feet high, it was a formidable obstacle. On the eastern end, local druggist John Carey Wolfe had built a mansion near the end of D Street. When the road was later extended south over the ridge to Ross Landing, it was called Wolfe Grade.

19

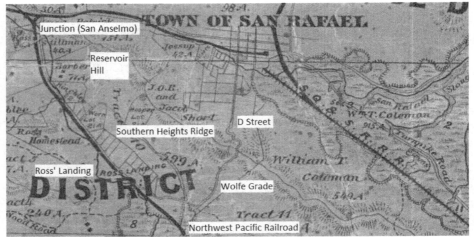

San Rafael and Ross before the road. On the 1873 map by Hiram Austin.

The only other existing route around the Heights was to take the San Rafael-Olema Road (now the Miracle Mile) west out of town, then turn south at Junction to Ross. This was nearly the same distance as Wolfe Grade, but it avoided the steep climb of the ridge.

Austin, however, decided to lay out the new road directly over the highest part of Southern Heights Ridge. The route would climb past the San Rafael Brewery at the end of Greenwood Avenue and come out at Ross. This new route was more direct but had so many twists it was only a tenth of a mile shorter than the existing routes. Clearly Austin meant to send the new road as directly as possible.

So Austin had his proposed route from San Rafael to Ross. From there he followed Lagunitas Road—Shaver's logging road—to the mouth of the canyon of Ross Creek. There were only two buildings on this dirt track, both catering to the hikers, ranchers, loggers, and hunters heading up into the back country. The first was a somewhat disreputable tavern called the Pink Saloon, owned by French immigrant Joseph Escallier. He had been in court charged with selling unlicensed liquor (a hung jury), and was later fined $160 or the same number of days for gambling. Once Escallier turned in a bunko man named Ed "Slim" Williams for fleecing him of $100. On the same property was a house owned by Escallier's partner, a Mrs. Smith. According to rumor, the two provided other services as a brothel servicing the loggers in the gulch above. The upright citizens of Ross fought against the place, and finally in 1891 it was purchased by Sheriff James Tunstead and Ross became a

dry town. The Pink Saloon found new life and respectability as the
Lagunitas Country Club.

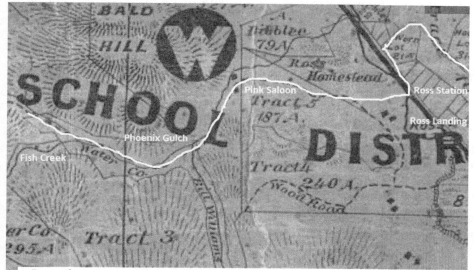

Route from Ross to Phoenix Gulch added to 1873 map of Marin by Hiram Austin.

Austin and his crew followed Lagunitas Road west up into the scenic
bowl of Phoenix Gulch, surrounded by steep forested slopes towering up
to the very summit of Mount Tamalpais. This little valley, possibly
named for the family of James Phenix, was then owned by the Marin
County Water Company, though it would be a quarter century before
they created Phoenix Lake on the site.

To get out of Phoenix Gulch, Shaver's logging road went up the steep
ravine of the south fork of Phoenix Creek to reach the divide above
Lagunitas Valley. The road sometimes followed the creek-bed and
sometimes clung precariously high above. This stretch, known as Shaver
Grade, was clearly going to be a challenge.

The party crossed a divide at 750 feet elevation and started down into
the valley of Lagunitas Creek. The route (now Bon Tempe Road)
descended past a small lake[7] to the Lagunitas Dairy established in 1858
by Colonel Archibald McDuff (1810-1882) and his wife, the widow Mrs.
Lucinda Messer. The dairy ranch produced 10,000 pounds of butter and
included 8 horses, 75 milk cows, 4 working oxen, 221 other cattle, and
40 swine. This area is now called Bullfrog at the upper tip of Alpine

---

[7] Now at the southeastern corner of the Meadow Club Golf Course.

Lake. In 1861, a ranch employee named Henry Chaffin reported trapping thirty-four bears and a mountain lion there in three years. Mr. King, his neighbor towards the future site of Lake Lagunitas, cut 600 cords of wood.[8]

Around 1868, McDuff sold his 1,180-acre ranch to David Porter, who then leased it to the Italian-Swiss brothers Joseph and Pasqual Bautumpi. Their dairy had 88 cows and provided butter to San Rafael, San Quentin prison, and the U.S. Army. Locals changed the name to Bontempi, or "good times." When Austin came through in 1878, the water company had just bought the land, but it would be another seventy years before they built Bon Tempe Dam, misspelling the name yet again—and obliterating the site of the dairy.

From this point Professor Austin laid out the alternate route to Fairfax. It climbed over the ridge to the north and dropped steeply down into the valley of San Anselmo Creek (now Sky Oaks Road), coming out at the gate into the Jory Ranch. From there it clung high on the side of the valley and descended a hogback to the railroad station in Fairfax (now the Parkade).

Returning to the Lagunitas Dairy, Austin followed Shaver's road westward down the valley of Lagunitas Creek. They passed through another dairy run by Vincent and Mary Jane Liberty, then continued down the creek to the junction of Lagunitas and Cataract Creeks. In 1865 Isaac Shaver and Jonathan Mitchner had leased a large tract of redwoods and firs here. They brought in a steam sawmill and built a handful of houses for the loggers and mill workers. In its heyday the mill produced sixteen thousand board-feet of lumber daily, which was hauled out to Ross Landing to be shipped to San Francisco. Eventually the huge old trees were cleared out. Shaver closed his mill in 1873 and moved the equipment into town, but the buildings were still there. This area is now known as Alpine, but it was apparently not called that until the 20th century, when Alpine Dam was built there. For the sake of clarity I will call it Alpine throughout.

Austin knew his road had to leave the valley here. They had been descending an easy grade ever since crossing the divide at the top of Shaver Grade. Now they needed to climb Bolinas Ridge. There are no gaps in this massive ridge, no passes or gradually rising canyons suitable for a road.

---

[8] *Ag & Industry Schedules* 1860.

As the little survey crew peered up from the canyon floor, the east face of the ridge soared a thousand feet in just under a mile—a daunting 38% grade. A wagon road could not exceed 8%, and preferably not more than 6%. Worse, the ridge was densely covered with redwood and Douglas firs and the precipitous slopes were deep in needle duff, bracken, and fallen branches to a depth of many feet, often over a man's head. Footing was treacherous, and it was difficult just to stand still without sliding down the slope.

The only existing path over this ridge was the old Indian trail from Bolinas to San Rafael. Built in ancient times by the San Rafael Miwoks to trade with their kin in villages at Bolinas, it had been used by the Spanish, Mexicans, and the early American settlers. But the old trail was so steep it was difficult to take a horse over it, and impossible for a wheeled vehicle. The hogback it descended on the far side, between Morse's Gulch and Weeks' Gulch, was far too narrow and precipitous for a road that could be used by wagons and coaches. A new route would have to be blazed. As he had at Southern Heights Ridge, Austin chose the most direct.

Crossing the creek, Austin sent his men scrambling up this slope, exploring various possible routes. The best of a bad lot was to ascend Cataract Canyon (then known as Whitney Gulch) as far as practical, then cross Cataract Creek and turn northwest to find a way out of the canyon.

When Austin's team finally clawed their way to the summit, they found themselves on a narrow, heavily-forested plateau running along the top of the ridge. Walking among the boles of the giant trees, their footsteps silent in the deep redwood duff, they emerged at the edge of yet another precipitous slope. The Pacific Ocean stretched to the distant horizon, broken only by the jagged crags of the Farallon Islands. Directly below them was Bolinas Lagoon, with their destination on the peninsula beyond. Their goal was only three miles away, but it was also 1500 feet below them—and the western face of the ridge was nearly as steep as the east.

Again they spread out, with teams clambering down each canyon and the hogbacks between. Every attempt led to some impossible difficulty, however, and they were forced to return to camp tired and covered in sweat and scratches. They worked their way northwest along the ridge more than two miles, crossing the heads of Bourne and Thompson Gulches (now Picher and Garden Club Canyons), both too steep for their purposes, before striking Pike County Gulch. Finally, after many exhausting climbs down and back up the ridge, Austin decided they would attempt to go down the hogback just beyond Pike County Gulch.

Austin's men chopped their way down through the dense forests. After many hours, the slope finally started to lessen. They crossed a low swampy area adjoining the head of Bolinas Lagoon—no doubt a trial for surveyor and stake driver alike. At last they hacked through a grove of willows and clambered up onto the Olema-Bolinas road about two miles north of Bolinas. The job had taken them just a week.

Austin reported his findings to the Board of Supervisors on Monday, June 4, 1877:

> The Bolinas Road. —At the last session of the Board of Supervisors, Surveyor Austin filed his report on the preliminary survey of the road over Tamalpais to Bolinas. It will be taken up at the next regular meeting. We have not the report at hand, but we understand the estimated cost to be quite low, somewhere about $4,000. A new petition is being circulated, and numerously signed, to secure the work. The people of Bolinas think their wishes should be regarded in this matter. They pay taxes on the railroad, without benefit from it, and they are isolated from the world.
>
> This road would bring all their traffic and travel through San Rafael, as it would bring them nearer to us than they are to Saucelito, and by an easier route. The benefit to San Rafael would be very considerable, and we have no doubt the people here would subscribe one-fourth of the expense. But friends of the road have mooted a scheme which seems to us wise. They propose to secure the right of way, and build a saddle trail over it. This done, the feasibility of the enterprise could be easily demonstrated. To secure the work, it must be shown that it will not be as expensive as was at first thought.
>
> *Marin County Journal*, 28 June 1877

Nothing came of this saddle trail plan. On August 9, 1877, the Board of Supervisors officially appointed Hiram Austin, Peter B. Whitney and William Blodgett as Road Viewers: a committee of three men—one of whom must be a licensed surveyor—assigned to lay out a proposed road and estimate the costs of acquiring the rights of way and building the road. To do this, they would have to do a detailed survey of every foot of the route.

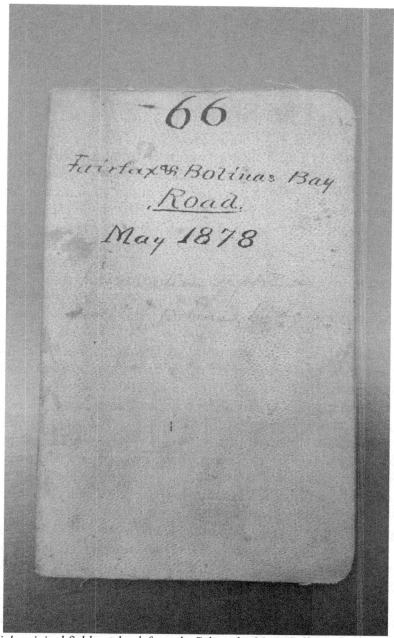

Austin's original field notebook from the Schroeder Maps Collection. Courtesy of the California Room at the Marin County Free Library.

The Survey, 1877

Survey work in the 19th century was heavy labor. Austin's theodolite was a precision instrument that had to be handled with extreme care. A hard bump could knock the setting circles out of alignment or damage the delicate optics. It was also heavy and required a solid tripod. Hauling such an instrument through thick forests while clambering over rocks and slipping down precipitous slopes required both delicacy and strength. His assistants carried the rod—a sixteen-and-a-half-foot graduated pole—which was also extremely awkward to carry through difficult country. The chains for measuring distance consisted of one hundred heavy steel links, each 7.92 inches long, totaling precisely sixty-six feet.

In practice, Austin would set up his tripod over a fixed point and center and level his theodolite. He would use a compass to precisely set the initial direction. He measured the height of the instrument above the point. A rodman would then walk out a reasonable distance, drive a stake into the ground at the center line of the proposed road, and hold his rod perfectly vertical over the new mark. Austin would sight the rod through the telescope and note the exact direction to the mark and where his level sight struck the rod so he could calculate the difference in elevation. His crew used the chain and plumb bobs to measure the distance to the mark, always ensuring that the chain was perfectly level and pulled with just the right tension to give an accurate distance. Austin would record all these figures in his notebook, adding descriptions and sketches as necessary. Then they would move the theodolite to the new mark and do reciprocal sights back to the first, confirming the distance, elevation, and angle against the first measurements. If the numbers differed, they had to go back and measure again to see which was correct. The result was a single dot added to the map.

They repeated this process every few hundred feet. In thick brush, sharp curves, or on steep slopes where they couldn't get a good line of sight between the points, the marks might be only feet apart.

Austin had to calculate the slope of the proposed road so it didn't exceed a reasonable grade for horses drawing wagons or coaches. At every creek crossing, he would calculate the size and location of any needed culvert or bridge. He computed the amount of rock and soil that would have to be cut or filled. They often had to clear brush, cut a path, or saw down trees to get a clear line of sight. They carried shovels, saws, sledgehammers, pry bars, hundreds of wooden stakes and metal spikes and pins, plus all their camping gear, clothing, food, and water. It was hot, hard, heavy work, and they worked long hours to take advantage of the long summer days. When they finally knocked off each day, they had to go back and break camp, pack all their equipment on the animals, ride a few miles, and make a new camp. This was in August, when temperatures might exceed a hundred degrees. And remember, Hiram Austin was fifty-seven and a very fat man.

The road from San Rafael to Ross would be a separate survey and construction project. So Austin's crew started in the settlement of Ross:

Beginning at a point in the West line of the County Road which runs from Red Hill to Ross Landing. Said place of beginning being the point at which the centre line of the road known as the Lagunitas Road intersects said West line of said road running from Red Hill to Ross Landing. Running thence from said place of beginning along the centre of said Lagunitas Road, crossing the tract of land known as Mrs Ross' homestead by the following courses and distances

1 S 78¼ W 781 feet.
2 S 66¼ W.33 "
3 S 61¼ W ?3 "
4 S 56¼ W 33 "
5 S 46¼ W 33 "

The first entries of Austin's official survey, from Marin County records.

Bearings were measured to a quarter of a degree and distances to the foot. The survey line marked the center line of a right of way sixty feet wide. As seen in the table, the first sight was a long straight shot of 781 feet down Lagunitas Road, as Shaver's logging road was called in Ross. Then the road had a sharp curve to the south, requiring a whole series of twelve short shots of only 33 feet each, or a half chain. This resulted in the first dots along the route of the new road:

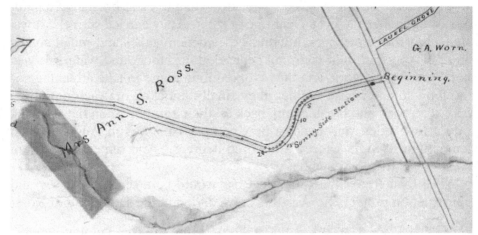

Detail from Austin's working map in the Schroeder Maps Collection.
Courtesy of the California Room of the Marin County Free Library.

They passed the Pink Saloon and crossed the rancho of Mrs. Ann S. Ross, James' widow, then worked their way up Ross Creek into Phoenix Gulch. The valley here was relatively level and open grasslands, so Austin was basically just mapping the existing logging road.

Shaver Grade

But the western side of Phoenix Gulch was a precipitous ridge that had to be surmounted to reach the higher country beyond. Phoenix Creek and Fish Creek (named for F. W. Fish, a former owner) descended the ridge in tumbling cataracts through steep gorges and joined to form Ross Creek. Parts of the logging road ran in the bed of the south fork of Phoenix Creek. This portion of the old road, known as Shaver Grade, was clearly much too narrow and boulder-strewn for a stagecoach road. Fish Gulch to the south was no better.

After studying the options, Austin decided to avoid this difficult stretch by crossing the creek and sending the new road up the northern fork of Phoenix Creek, taking a longer route and climbing steeply to a point now known as Five Corners, then curling around to the west, where it rejoined Shaver's road. This new route would become known as the new Shaver Grade and the old Shaver Grade fell into disuse. It is now known as Logging Trail.

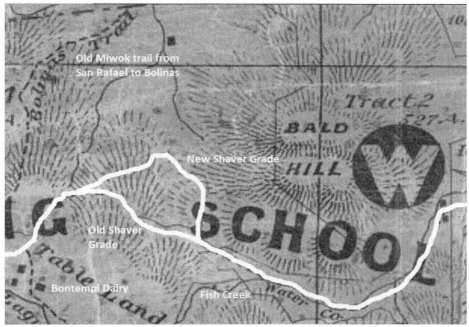

Route from Phoenix Gulch to Bontempi added to 1873 map of Marin by Hiram Austin.

Climbing over a divide at 800 feet elevation, Austin's crew dropped into the watershed of Lagunitas Creek, fed by dozens of springs and small streams flowing down the north side of Tamalpais. The water company had bought this valley in 1871, and the following year built Lagunitas Dam at the upper end, creating the beautiful—if redundantly named—Lake Lagunitas to supply water to San Rafael. Austin's road stayed well north of the lake, winding around the north side of a round-topped mountain and dropping down into Bontempi Ranch, now owned by the water company.

Austin and his crew then turned north to survey the route to Fairfax, descending the steep hogback above San Anselmo Creek. When they completed this route to the Fairfax railroad station, they retraced their steps to the Bontempi Dairy to begin the route down the Lagunitas Valley.

Descending from the dairy, the road followed the right bank of the creek as it meandered southwest down a broad valley through sunny meadows dotted with herds of deer, elk, and an occasional bear or mountain lion. On their left, a handful of hunting and fishing cabins lay in the deep shade under the towering redwood trees along the creek, seen against a nearly vertical two-thousand-foot ridge, a dark green wall of immense firs forming the north flank of Tamalpais. The survey work would have gone quickly down this valley.

They left the land owned by the water company and entered that of the wealthy and powerful Shafter-Howard family. On their right Liberty Creek came down out of the hills to join the main creek. This was the site of Liberty Ranch. Behind the ranch, a pair of wagon ruts wound up the long narrow canyon and disappeared into the darkness beneath the big trees. Cattle grazed on the wildflowers in the meadow. This was the entrance to Curtis Gulch, named after Loomis Curtis.

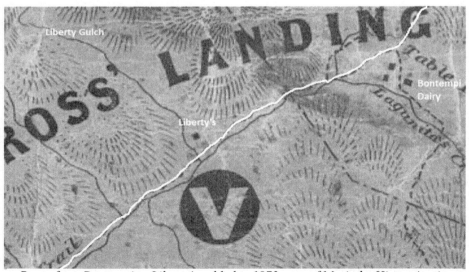

Route from Bontempi to Liberty's added to 1873 map of Marin by Hiram Austin.

Loomis and Elizabeth Curtis

Loomis Curtis was born in Springfield, New York in 1827 and came to Olema in 1857. He worked on dairy ranches in Point Reyes, and in 1864 married Elizabeth McGovern and they had three children, Ella, Mary and Frank. By 1867 he was a dairyman in Bolinas. Then he and Elizabeth leased the canyon in Lagunitas from the Shafter-Howard family and established an 1,100-acre dairy there. He became an invalid at age 43 and suffered severe discomfort and many business reverses. He had to give up ranching in 1870 and moved to Martinez. Loomis died in Stockton in 1875 at age 49. His wife Elizabeth tried to keep the dairy running, but with three small children and no help she was forced to auction off all of the dairy fixtures and stock in September 1876, amounting to 64 milk cows, some cattle, and a few horses and hogs, along with the farming and dairying equipment. She and the children moved to San Rafael.

Liberty Ranch. Courtesy of Jack Mason Museum of West Marin History

Vincent and Mary Jane Liberty

Vincent Liberty was born to French immigrants in Canada in 1837. In the 1850s he came to California and by 1860 was working as a farm laborer in San Rafael. The next year he trapped a bear on a ranch where he worked in San Geronimo, probably the White Rancho owned by Adolph Mailliard. On April 7, 1866, aged 29, he married Mary Jane Hancorn, 24, at the Cosmopolitan Hotel in San Francisco. The next year they had a daughter Elodia Josephine, and in 1868 a son Vincent Henry, Jr., known as Vinnie. In 1870 they were in Nicasio Township, where they bought a thousand acres of dairy land near Mount Barnabe from Adolph Mailliard for $16,590. When Elizabeth Curtis had to give up the dairy, Vincent Liberty leased the land and moved his family there, and from that day on it has been known as Liberty Gulch. In 1875, they had another son, Leland Leslie.

On January 12, 1878, their oldest son Vinnie, nine years old, went down to William Anderson's slaughterhouse at 3rd and B Streets in San Rafael to watch the men scalding the carcass of a hog:

> Last Saturday, just at night, Vincent H., oldest son of Mr. and Mrs. Vincent Liberty, went down to Anderson's slaughter house, with Mr. Thomas Hilton, and while there, in passing the vats of hot water, by a misstep, he fell in, and was scalded. The scalding was not sufficient to produce death, but he had just recovered from typhoid fever, and the shock to his nervous system was so great that he died at nine o'clock the next morning. He was a fine bright, manly lad, fond of his books, affectionate, and obedient, and a favorite with all who knew him.
>
> *Marin County Journal*, 17 January 1878

Another account says the boy was immersed to the waist and lingered in agony for days. It must have been an excruciating experience for all.

There were apparently many bears on the Liberty Ranch. On September 5, 1878, the *Marin County Journal* reported:

> Big Bear—A powerful heavy specimen of bear meat stopped at Obitz' shop last Sunday, whence it was sent to the city. It was a cinnamon, but so dark as to be mistaken for a black by some. It weighed 340 pounds, and would have made short work with a man in close quarters. It was killed by Vincent Liberty, who decoyed it with the carcass of an animal, though the feat has been credited to some amateur sportsmen at the Tamalpais.

A lady reader of the *Journal* has had grave doubts in her mind as to the truth of our statements about bears killed on Tamalpais, and the tracks of a California lion, nine inches around, being seen on a ranch near here. So the other day when Vincent Liberty brought in a bruin's carcass, a friend took her down to see it, and she said she would never doubt us again.

In addition to the milk cows they grazed in Lagunitas Valley, the Libertys also kept herds over the ridge to the northwest in Little Carson Canyon. They used teams of oxen to drag the milk on wooden sledges down the steep slopes to the dairy (the track is now the Old Sled Trail).

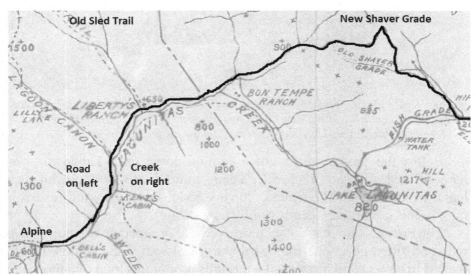

Route of the road shown on a detail from a 1902 Sanborn tourists' map.

Lagunitas Canyon

Laying out the new road past Liberty Ranch, Austin's survey party continued southwest down Lagunitas Canyon. Directly across the creek from the ranch was a cabin owned by the Hoffman family. On their right, Lagoon Canyon (named for tiny Lily Lake, now mostly silted in) sent another stream to join Lagunitas Creek. Austin noted yet another bridge that would have to be built. Just beyond on the far side of the creek was Johnson's Lagunitas Rancho. And just below was a cabin belonging to

33

the wealthy family of Albert Emmett Kent, who owned large tracts of land and for whom Kentfield is named.

Albert Kent's hunting cabin beside Lagunitas Creek. Note the deer hanging in the tree. Photo courtesy of William Kent Family Papers (MS 309), Manuscripts and Archives, Yale University Library. Image copied by Tim Wood.

Below the Kent cabin, a gulch coming down from Tamalpais was named Swede George Gulch, after a deaf-mute Swedish logger who once had a cabin there[9]. The water company had a small dam and reservoir high in this gulch (now destroyed by a landslide).

The broad Lagunitas Valley narrowed and dropped down into a steep redwood-filled gorge. A major tributary, Cataract Creek, entered from the left in a spectacular series of waterfalls dropping a total of a thousand feet.

A man named F. C. Peters[10] had built a cabin beside the creek here, and had put a lot of work into beautifying the place. He'd piped the creek water into a watering trough with a bucket for the use of passers-by. He'd built two graceful suspension bridges across the creeks and had rolled rocks into the Lagunitas to form a swimming hole and propped up the branches of the trees so they formed a scenic bower over the pool.

---

[9] He was born around 1835 in New York and came to California in 1863. He lived alone in his canyon, cutting wood for saddle trees, until he suffered a stroke and became partially paralyzed. He was ensconced in a rough cabin on the courthouse lawn, a ward of the state. He died in April 1875, but no one ever learned his name.

[10] Frederick Cornelius Peters (1848-1938).

The entrance to this idyllic spot was a handsome red-painted gate between stone pillars.

Route from Alpine to Bolinas added to 1873 map of Marin by Hiram Austin
Also shows the old Bolinas and San Rafael Trail.

Bolinas Ridge

Austin and his crew crossed Lagunitas creek and started up Cataract Canyon. Until now, except for the new Shaver Grade, they had merely been mapping the existing rutted dirt tracks used by the loggers. Their gear and supplies accompanied them in wagons. Now they were cutting a new trail through thick forest. All the gear had to be hauled up the hill on their horses and mules, and much of the time on their backs. How the portly Hiram Austin and his crew managed to climb this wall, dragging their survey instruments, plane tables, rods and chains, levels and plumb bobs, food and supplies and animals, is hard to conceive. They not only made the difficult climb successfully, they surveyed and mapped a feasible route, involving two and a half miles of the most twisting route imaginable, with fifty sharp curves bringing the average grade down to 8%, barely possible for teams of horses.

Following the tree blazes made in the preliminary survey, they worked their way northwest along the top of the ridge. They then started the long descent. The slope was so steep they had to repeatedly survey the line up and over a rocky ridge, where the road would later be blasted through it. Austin had to plot the route so that the amount of rock excavated would roughly equal the required fill. He continued to add to his list of bridges and culverts and watering troughs to be built. When they reached the foot of the grade, they still had to cross the marsh before they could stand on the Olema-Bolinas Road—tired, scratched, and no doubt relieved.

Then, after transporting the crew and remaining supplies back to San Rafael, Austin still had a great deal to do. He had to type up his list of hundreds of surveyed points and add all his comments and descriptions: dead redwood, nail in tree, 12x12" redwood culvert, bridge 20 feet.

For every bridge, he provided very detailed specifications. For the bridge over Cataract Creek, he said: "Needs a bridge fifty feet long between abutments. Bridge to be built on the same plan as Bridge #1 and to be sixteen feet wide. The rock at each end of the bridge is to be cleared off and made in good shape to receive the abutments which shall be built up of flattened redwood timbers of at least 18 inches face and to be bolted at each end of the bridge with 4½" iron bolts running down into the solid rock at least 1½ feet. Each bolt to be wedged or leaded into the rock." Some of these specifications went on for pages.

Then he drew up a new map, entering all his hundreds of numbered points. When his final hand-drawn map was complete, he proudly signed his name: "H. Austin, Surveyor."

P LAT

Of the Fairfax & Bolinas Bay Road,

~~OF THE SAN RAFAEL AND BOLINAS ROAD~~

PETITIONED FOR BY A D. EASKOOT AND OTHERS

SURVEYED BY ORDER OF THE BOARD OF SUPERVISORS OF MARIN CO

SCALE 600 FEET TO AN INCH.

MAG. VAR. 16° E.

SURVEY COMMENCED AUGUST 13° 1877

H. Austin Surveyor

Title from Austin's original survey map from the Schroeder Maps Collection.
Courtesy of the California Room at the Marin County Free Library.

Note that the name of the road was changed from San Rafael to Fairfax. This seems odd, as the supervisors had asked for a road to Fairfax, and Austin gave them roads to both Fairfax and San Rafael.

On September 13, 1877, Austin presented his report to the Board of Supervisors. The Board accepted the plans and authorized payment to Austin of $250 for his survey. His assistants Whitney and Blodgett received $57 and $68.44 for their part. So the County paid $375 for the survey, for which they had budgeted no more than $70. They accepted Austin's recommendation to build the road to San Rafael rather than Fairfax.

When the Board began to discuss the construction of the road in November, several landowners objected, saying they should be paid damages for their lost land. Some of these were signers of the petition requesting the road. The *Marin County Journal* decried their actions:

The proposed road over Mount Tamalpais, to give direct communication between San Rafael and Bolinas, was considered in the Board of Supervisors last week, and will be taken up again on Tuesday, 27th instant. Several parties indicated a desire for damages, in amounts which, if they are pressed, will probably defeat the measure. But we hope a liberal policy will be pursued on both sides, that a work of such great public utility may be secured. The road will be of incalculable benefit to both Bolinas and San Rafael. It will be to Bolinas what the railroad is to Olema; and the addition of such a splendid drive to the present attractions of San Rafael will increase its fame many fold. The matchless scenery from its heights, and its terminus on the sea, will make it one of the most attractive and famous pleasure rides in the country. Property holders and business men in San Rafael cannot afford to allow its defeat.

Marin County Journal, 15 November 1877

The Shafter-Howards

The biggest landowners along the route, indeed in the county, were the Shafter-Howard family. The Shafter brothers were born in Vermont and came to California in 1856. They were wealthy attorneys in San Francisco and politically active and powerful.

Oscar Lovell Shafter (1812-1873) served on the Oakland city council and was also appointed judge. In 1840 Oscar married 17-year-old Sarah Riddle (1823-1900) and she gave him ten daughters and one son. His law firm acquired the entire peninsula of Point Reyes and the lands there were divided into the "alphabet" dairy ranches that continue to this day. In 1864 he was appointed an associate justice of the California Supreme Court, but he fell ill and had to retire. He went to Europe to recover his health, but died in Florence in 1873. After his death, his wife Sarah sued for and won the rights to his vast land holdings, estimated to be worth over a million dollars—twenty million in today's money.

Oscar Lovell Shafter

Oscar's brother James McMillan Shafter (1816-1892), four years younger, had been a state legislator in their native Vermont, and later Secretary of State. In 1845 he married Julia Granville Hubbard (1822-1871). He moved to Wisconsin and became Speaker of the Assembly there. In 1856 he moved to California and joined a law partnership with his brother. He was appointed judge of the Superior Court, was President Pro Tem of the California Senate, and a regent of the University of California.

James McMillan Shafter

Oscar's youngest daughter Emma married another wealthy landowner, Charles Webb Howard, and he joined in the family business of buying land and building dairy ranches. He became president of the Spring Valley Water Company. Between the three of

Emma Lovell Shafter

them—Sarah, James, and Charles—they owned a good portion of Marin County, including much of the Lagunitas watershed where the proposed road was to be built.

The family sued the County, the water company, and the railroads many times over the decades, usually for real or perceived damages, and they remained a problem for the authorities through the rest of the century.

But in this case, after several hearings and over the owners' objections, the supervisors voted to condemn the right-of-way through the various properties. The owners all received compensation, but the Shafter-Howards were dissatisfied with the amount.

Now that the right-of-way was acquired, the project could move forward. As always with public projects, it then became a matter of paying for it.

Charles Webb Howard

The Funding, 1878

Funding for the project was a major topic and, as new tax revenue was clearly required, the issue went to the state legislature. In February 1878, Assemblyman Charles D. Allen introduced a bill to authorize the Board of Supervisors to levy a special tax of five cents on every $100 of assessed property, for three years. The bill stated that the new tax was "to build a public highway from Bolinas Bay to the Olema and San Rafael Road, or to the Ross Valley road, as may be determined." It was estimated that the tax would raise about $12,000, and the road was projected to cost no more than $10,000.

On February 7th, the *Journal* opined:

> The present Board of Supervisors is composed of three as careful, economical and conservative men as could be picked out in the county[11]. Not one of them is in the jobbing line, and neither of them can be hoodwinked by anyone disposed to speculate on works of a public character. A road hence to Bolinas is a work imperatively demanded. The grade on the projected route will be easier than the Saucelito road, and only half the distance. We have heard of no opposition to it, and have talked with many citizens from points not directly benefitted by the road, who all favor the project. We therefore hope the bill will pass without opposition, and the work be speedily pushed to completion.

But there was still opposition in some quarters:

> We understand that the bill to authorize the Board of Supervisors to build a road from this place to Bolinas Bay is being opposed by some gentlemen in Saucelito. We regret to hear this, because it is a measure of great public advantage. It will lessen the distance to the growing town of

---

[11] John Charles Gibson (1828-1893), chairman; William Rowland (1824-1923) and John William Atherton (1835-1911), associates.

Bolinas more than one-half, and give a much easier grade than the old route. Bolinas is entitled to the best facilities of communication that it is possible to give her. She is twelve miles from the railroad, and 27 to 30 miles from the county seat by wagon. The proposed road will bring her within 15 miles of this place, and by a route much easier to travel than the old one. The voice of Saucelito is the only one that has been heard in opposition to the measure, and the only ground for that must be, that the new route will divert some of the travel from passing through that town. We would remind Saucelito that when they wanted a road opened to Bolinas, the county promptly gave it to them; and will they be less magnanimous with others?

Marin County Journal, 21 February 1878

Some opponents of the project wrote indignant letters to the editor:

Ed. *Journal:* Dear Sir - I see by the *Journal* of February 21st that "Bolinas is entitled to the best facilities of communication that it is possible to give her." Why is she so entitled? Is it because by building a road for her it will help to build up San Rafael, and also enhance the property of a few bloated land holders along the line of the proposed road? And the rest of the county are to bear the burden—or the greater portion of it—for a road which they will never travel nor have any interest in. There are some old residents hereabouts that have been heard to say they "have not forgotten how it has been in times past." They have wanted roads, and our county fathers were magnanimous enough to grant Saucelito and Bolinas one, and let others go without. It is certain that three-fourths of the taxpayers here would readily sign a protest against the pet "Bolinas Road Bill," and, if I am not greatly in error, the road districts north of us would do the same; or perhaps go further, and sign unanimously. Oh, no! We do not feel like paying five mills on the one hundred dollars, when we have to travel roads that are in such condition that the drowning of a team or the breaking of a wagon is of daily occurrence.

"Nicasio"
Marin County Journal, 28 February 1878

But most residents seemed to be in favor of the new road. Bolinas and San Rafael, the towns that would gain the most benefit, together represented over twenty percent of the county population and both strongly supported the project.

In the spring, the road bill passed the legislature and was signed into law. With funding finally secured, in May the Board authorized the road, though there was still debate about its exact route. Supervisor John C. Gibson authorized another survey of the route between the Bolinas Ridge and the Olema-San Rafael Road, in search of a cheaper alternative. There was talk of moving the eastern terminus back to Fairfax, but it was decided to accept Austin's proposal.

On June 3rd, 1878, the Board requested bids to construct the new road. The road from San Rafael to Ross would be built by Robert Makin as a separate project. The road from Ross to Bolinas was divided into five sections:

Section One: from Ross through Phoenix Gulch, up Shaver Grade, through Bontempi and Liberty Ranches, and down the valley of Lagunitas Creek to Alpine at the eastern base of Bolinas Ridge. This section was by far the longest, but presented fewer engineering problems—6¼ miles.

Section Two: from Alpine up Cataract Gulch to the start of the steepest part of Bolinas Ridge—1½ miles.

Section Three: from that point to the top of Bolinas Ridge—1½ miles.

Section Four: from the top of the ridge to the top of Pike County Gulch—2 miles.

Section Five: the descent down Pike County Gulch to Bolinas Lagoon—2¾ miles.

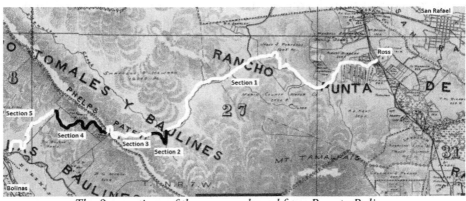

The five sections of the proposed road from Ross to Bolinas

The overall length was around 14 miles. Contractors could bid on any or all sections, but they would have to submit a $100 certified check for each section they bid on. The county would pay for the work in gold and silver coin, half and half. Bids would be accepted up to noon on the 24th of June and the work had to be completed by the first of December.

Before any bids were even submitted, a new controversy arose:

Bolinas Road in Danger.—Matters have progressed favorably in the matter of opening the Bolinas and San Rafael road, and the Supervisors last week advertised for bids on the contracts for work. Within the past few days, however, new complications have arisen touching the right of way, and there is great danger that the grand enterprise will be defeated, or at least delayed for a long time. The road is a work of great public importance, pregnant with benefits for all interests on its line, but it can be defeated for the present, if a liberal policy is not pursued.

Marin County Journal, 13 June 1878

It is unclear what the problem was with the right-of-way. But months later the Board of Supervisors approved some large payments to the Shafter-Howard family, so perhaps this is how the issue was resolved.

It seemed that, after all the discussion and debate, the road was finally going to be built. But the controversy had only just begun. Now the issue became, who would do the work? And this question nearly led to outright armed violence.

The Bidding, 1878

Over the next three weeks, four sealed proposals were submitted to the office of the clerk of the Board of Supervisors, each accompanied by the appropriate deposit. On Monday, June 24th, 1878, the bidding was closed, and the following day the bids were opened and read by the Supervisors. They were as follows:

Colwell & Wilkins—For Section Two, $3,445; Section Three, $2,195; Section Four, $2,195; Section Five, $2,145.

Wm. M. Blodgett et al—Section Five only, $2,472.

Lemon & Wing—Section One, $2,700; Sections Two, Three, Four and Five, $9,000.

Redfield & Mier—For all five sections, earthwork and bridges, $26,615.

Redfield and Mier's price was twice the other bids and was quickly eliminated. Blodgett's bid for Section Five was higher than Colwell & Wilkins' bid for that section, so it too was rejected. That left just two contractors in contention. Colwell's total bid was $9,980 for just four of the sections. Assuming Section One would cost two to three thousand, the whole job would be well over $12,000.

Lemon & Wing's bid for the entire road was $11,700. Clearly, they were the lowest bidders. They were a well-established company from San Diego and had built several large projects, including a major levee in Sutter County and a narrow-gauge railroad between Vacaville and Winters. Both county policy and the state road bill authorizing the project clearly specified that the county had to accept the lowest bid, but there was an unforeseen problem.

Lemon and Wing were Chinese.

Marin County, like much of the rest of the country, was deeply racist. This was long before the days of political correctness, and newspapers routinely published cruel racial jokes and derogatory comments about blacks, the Irish, and Latinos. But the most hated and feared were Asians.

They looked different, they talked differently, most were not Christians, few could speak any but the most broken English, and they were routinely considered sub-human. Thousands of Asians had come over to the U.S during the gold rush, and many more were brought in as cheap labor to build the railroads. Now many of them were out of work. Chinese exclusion laws barred them from undertaking most businesses, and systemic racism prevented them from entering American society.

Card for the Workingmen's Party of California. Found in a survey index book of George Dodge, Schroeder Maps Collection, Marin County Free Library.

They had little choice but to take any work offered them, no matter how poor the pay.

There were numerous anti-Chinese and anti-Japanese societies dedicated to driving all Asians from the country. They held open meetings that were announced in the papers like any other social event. Violence against Asians was common and rarely punished. Most residents of Marin were opposed to having Asians in the county at all, much less getting contracts and jobs in place of whites. The Board of

Supervisors knew they could not let the job to Chinese contractors. They would be run out of office, and possibly the county. They adjourned without a decision and scheduled another meeting the following day, Wednesday, June 26.

There must have been some interesting discussions in the Board room in the County Courthouse that warm June afternoon as the three Supervisors tried to find a way out of their predicament. The minutes of the meeting do not record these arguments. In the end, they say only:

> The bids from the different parties for building the Bolinas and Fairfax Road, secured and examined by this Board, after due consideration, it is ordered by the Board that each and all of said Bids be and are hereby rejected.

Road Minutes, Wednesday, June 26, 1878

There was no public announcement of why all the bids were rejected and the newspapers did not comment on it. But how could the road be built?

There is no documentation, but we can imagine the Supervisors calling in Colwell and Wilkins for a closed meeting and telling them of their problem. The Chinese bid for Sections Two through Five was $9,000, almost a thousand under their own bid. That was clearly unacceptable. Could Colwell and Wilkins possibly see their way to reducing their bid to below that of the Chinese? Section One could be done later under a separate contract, and the Board could sweeten that deal so Colwell and Wilkins could recoup their losses.

The two partners must have gone through their figures, trying to pare down their estimate by over a thousand dollars. We don't know what deals and promises were made on either side, but a week later a deal was reached.

On the following Wednesday the contract was let to the relatively untried firm of Colwell & Wilkins for the sum of $8,500 (roughly $184,000 today), which was 15% less than their original bid. Unless that bid had been wildly overpriced, it is hard to see how they could hope to build the road at the new price. Nonetheless, the contract was drawn up and signed by both parties, and Colwell & Wilkins "filed a bond for $1,000.00 for the faithful performance of said contract."

We can only wonder what Lemon and Wing thought of this, for of course they knew they had been the lowest bidders—the bids were in the public record.

At last, construction of the Bolinas-San Rafael Road could begin. Although the Chinese question was far from resolved, Colwell and Wilkins had no time to waste.

The Builders

Jesse Colwell (1833-1899)

Jesse Colwell was born in Ohio in March 1833 and came to Marin in the 1850s, probably for the gold rush. The first official record of him is in December 1863, when he registered for the Civil War draft, though he apparently did not serve. At the time he was a 30-year-old unmarried farmer in Bolinas. He did not remain unmarried for long, for within a year, at age 32, he married Mary Jane Ingram. Just 22, she was the daughter of his neighbors Hugh and Jane Ingram, who had emigrated from County Armagh, Northern Ireland, in 1851. Jesse and Mary Jane were married on November 28, 1864, at the bride's parents' home in Bolinas.

Jesse and Mary Jane Colwell in 1860s, courtesy of the Jack Mason Museum of West Marin History.

The newlyweds lived on a ranch in Union Gulch, near the head of Bolinas lagoon, a site now on US-1. Jesse became a county clerk and a road contractor. In 1864 he built the White Hill Road[12] for $1,700. He was deputy sheriff for a while, but resigned in September 1865. In October 1866 they had their first

---

[12] The section of Sir Francis Drake Boulevard from Fairfax to the San Geronimo Valley.

child, a son named Grant. The day before Christmas 1867, they had another boy, Archie, and in May 1870 a third son, Victor Jesse.

Sometime in the 1870s the family left Bolinas and moved to San Rafael. Jesse, then 45, went into partnership with a Bolinas neighbor, James Wilkins, 27, as road contractors. In addition to his contracting work, Jesse became a guard at the penitentiary at San Quentin. After a gap of eight years, in 1878 Mary Jane finally gave Jesse a daughter, Idelle Marin, known as Ida.

In September 1883, Mary Jane was driving her mother Jane Ingram and her four-year-old daughter Ida home from Ross. They were at the present corner of Tunstead and Sir Francis Drake in San Anselmo when they heard a team overtaking them. Mary Jane pulled over to let them pass, but it was a runaway horse dragging a smashed buggy. The horse struck their carriage so hard all three were thrown forward out of the vehicle. The runaway horse went right over them. Mary Jane was knocked unconscious, Ida only bruised, but the horse stepped on the face of Jane Ingram and she died at the scene.

The children grew up in San Quentin and the boys were avid outdoorsmen, roaming and hunting the back country of Marin. The oldest son Grant was acknowledged the best sharpshooter and rider in the county.

The second son, Archie, at age sixteen got a job as assistant at the *Sausalito News*, but soon decided he wanted to go to sea. In January 1889, when he was 22, he signed on for a voyage to Alaska aboard the sealing schooner *O. S. Fowler*. On such voyages, the men received no wages, just shares of the profit from the seal, otter, and polar bear skins taken. The hunting season was in the winter and the work was extremely dangerous and difficult, but one successful voyage could yield enough to set a man up in business or to buy a home. With any luck, Archie would return a wealthy man. But he did not have luck. Only a few days after sailing from Sausalito, they put into Drake's Bay and a boat was launched to go ashore with young Archie at the tiller. The wind was high and the seas rough. The boat capsized and all three men were lost. His father Jesse spent weeks wandering the shores of Drake's Bay, searching for the body of his son. It was three weeks before he and one shipmate were found. The third body was not found for five months.

Undeterred by this tragedy, less than two years later Archie's older brother Grant, 25, signed on for a similar voyage aboard the sealing schooner *Mattie O. Dyer*. (We can only imagine what his parents thought of this decision.) But it was an unfortunate voyage, marred by bad luck, hardship and mutiny, and he received no wages.

The third son Victor started working in Gorley's Emporium in San Rafael[13]. By 1890, he was driving the stagecoach between Tocaloma and Olema. The railroad turned north to Cazadero at the big hotel at Tocaloma, so passengers bound to Bolinas got off the train there and took the stagecoach to Olema, where they could change to another stage to Bolinas. Victor was nineteen at the time, so this was a responsible position for him, but he was apparently successful:

Victor Colwell is the popular young driver of the Tocaloma and Olema stage.

Sausalito News, 19 December 1890

When the prospect of war with Spain became imminent, Grant Colwell wanted to serve his country. He joined the army and was selected for Teddy Roosevelt's Roughriders:

WITH ARIZONA COWBOYS.
Marin County Boy in Roosevelt's famous Company.

Grant Colwell, a brother of Miss Idelle Colwell of San Rafael, is one of the members of Roosevelt's cowboy company. As all the world knows, Roosevelt resigned his position as Assistant Secretary of War, to lead a company of "rough riders," as the cowboy companies are called, to the front. To recruit a regiment of these hardy and fearless fellows was a task of no small proportions, not that there was an insufficiency of brave boys, but the purpose was to select from the hundreds of applicants, only those who were expert with the lasso, pistol and rifle and who could manage any kind of horse under any conditions. That Grant Colwell was selected to join the company of rough riders is something that Marin County has reason to be proud of.

Sausalito News, 21 May 1898

Grant fought with distinction in Cuba, returned home briefly, and two years later fought in China against the Boxer Rebellion. His

---

[13] At 807 Fourth Street, now the Old San Rafael Mall.

descriptive letters home to his family were published in the papers and he was renowned as a war hero.

If Grant was a hero the family could look upon with pride, Victor took quite a different path. He was apparently a moody boy given to fits of depression. He developed a drinking problem. He lost his job with the stage line and spent some time in Sausalito, working as a brakeman on the railroad. With his brother fighting in Cuba, Victor tried to enlist as well, but the army turned him down, for reasons unrecorded. He became desperate, and as we shall see in a later chapter, turned to crime.

Jesse's daughter Ida was a deputy clerk in County Clerk Bonneau's office. In October 1897, as she was returning to the court house from lunch, she found a body sprawled against her office door. There had been a fight on the courthouse lawn over a woman, and the victim had fled into the courthouse for safety. But everyone was out for lunch, and his assailant caught him there and murdered him.

Ida was very talented and social. In the first decade of the new century she was in the papers every few weeks, attending various parties and balls, in vocal performances, and visiting friends and relatives. She was also a volunteer or officer in several church organizations.

James Hepburn Wilkins (1854-1934)

James Hepburn Wilkins, aged 66, from his 1920 passport application.

Jesse's partner James Hepburn Wilkins was born in Baltimore in 1854. He and his older brother Hepburn Wilkins (Hepburn was their mother's maiden name) came to Marin in 1863 with their parents. Their father Henry Wilkins was a prominent San Rafael attorney.

James Wilkins studied civil engineering at the University of California and then worked for the Southern Pacific Railroad. After forming his partnership with Jesse Colwell and completing the Bolinas-Fairfax and several other road-building projects, in 1879 he gave up construction and started the newspaper the *Marin County Tocsin* (he wrote the damning-with-faint-praise obituary of Hiram Austin). In 1884 he married Lucy Arrington in San Francisco, but the marriage must not have been successful, for only two years later he married Isabella G. Forbes. They had a daughter Lucille Forbes in 1888, a son James Hepburn, Jr. in 1899, and a second son Alexander Forbes in 1901. In 1885, Wilkins founded another newspaper, the *Sausalito News*.

In August 1917, shortly after the declaration of war against Germany, James Jr. enrolled in the army. Assigned to a headquarters unit, he asked to be transferred to the front and fought in many battles. Three months before the end of the war, on August 17, 1918, he attacked and captured a German machine-gun nest at Apremont in the Ardennes, France, but was killed in the process. Three years later, his body was returned to this country and buried with full military honors in Mount Tamalpais Cemetery.

James Sr. became the City Engineer for San Rafael and later the mayor. His was the first voice to seriously propose a bridge across the Golden Gate. He was the Director of the State Prison Board, and Folsom prison was built under his administration. In later years, he was a power in the Democratic Party in California and was elected to the State Assembly. His son Alexander was involved in an automobile accident in 1934 and suffered a head injury, causing amnesia. Soon after, Alexander wandered away from his home, wife, and children, and was never found. Apparently strongly affected by this incident, James Wilkins, 80, died November 10, 1934.

The Construction, 1878-1879

San Anselmo in 1869. Painting by William Keith.

After the bidding fiasco, Colwell and Wilkins were under pressure to deliver the project on time and under the very tight budget that had been forced on them.

It was going to be a big job, similar to a military expedition. They estimated the work would require 250 men for at least four months. The first step was to hire fifteen foremen—experts in blasting, excavating, hauling, building bridges, and so forth. Each would manage a group of ten to twenty laborers. The large labor force would require many wagons and carriages and scores of horses and oxen, along with drivers and hostlers and blacksmiths and wainwrights. All the tools and materials for the construction—picks and shovels and rock drills and tamping rods, and dynamite by the ton—would have to be delivered to the work site. They would need food and gear for camping, with the requisite dishes and food storage and cooks and dishwashers. The men would need guns for hunting, for the hills were full of deer and bear and they could feed the entire camp.

The materials were a fixed cost; they could not cut corners there. And the foremen had to be skilled and experienced. They were critical to the project's success, and had to be paid the going wage. The laborers were the one place they could cut costs. Quick calculations showed that the partners could not hope to break even if they paid more than $1.25 a day, a very low wage even then, equivalent to less than three dollars an hour today.

They knew that no self-respecting working man would take the job at those wages. There are no ads in the papers for these jobs. It was not publicly announced. Colwell and Wilkins did what many companies of the time did. Most likely the partners simply quietly approached Lemon and Wing and hired their workers. The work would be done by the Chinese after all.

They decided to start from the Bolinas end, with Section Five. The train of wagons must have looked like a military column as they rolled out of town, with 250 Chinese laborers, the foremen and managers, and all the supplies. They made their initial camp along the Olema-Bolinas Road just north of the bridge over Wilkins Creek, on the ranch of William Wallace Wilkins (1824-1911)—no relation to James Wilkins.

On Wednesday, July 17th, 1878, they began cutting the road up Pike County Gulch, following the stakes placed by Hiram Austin and his crew thirteen months earlier. The route roughly paralleled the old Indian trail in Weeks Gulch a mile and a half to the south. On July 18th, the *Marin County Journal* took note of the start of construction:

The Bolinas Road work was commenced yesterday, by Wilkins and Colwell. You can drive over it to the beach in about three months. At least, we hope so.

The first task was to build a short causeway across the marsh at the head of Bolinas Lagoon. Then they started up the hill. The grade at first was gentle and the work consisted of cutting down willow trees, hauling out the stumps, and leveling the roadway. But soon the road started climbing the Bolinas Ridge and blasting was required every few yards. Massive explosions thundered out, sending broken rock spinning down into the steep gulches. Local residents would turn at the sound of the blast and look up at the ridge, seeing clouds of dust rising from among the trees, revealing the progress of the road. They soon grew inured to the frequent thunder of dynamite.

The hillside faced the Pacific, and it was prone to extremely heavy rainfalls during the winter. Drainage always had to be considered, with ditches lining the road and frequent culverts and bridges to be built. At suitable spots, they built stonework watering troughs to catch the mountain freshets for the use of the horses that would soon be using the road. (Several of these are still visible today—and still full of water.) Jesse Colwell and Jim Wilkins must have been very busy managing this whole operation, ordering supplies as needed and ensuring they arrived at the right times. Still, the work went on, but very slowly—much slower than Colwell and Wilkins had planned.

Throughout July the road slowly advanced up the slope, switching back and forth as it climbed toward the summit. By early August, it had arrived at the top of Bolinas Ridge. They moved their supplies up the hill and set up a new camp under the huge redwoods there, generally out of sight of the Bolinas residents. Still, the workers frequently came down to Bolinas to purchase groceries and supplies for their camp.

Labor Trouble

Having large numbers of Chinese laborers in their midst was upsetting to the citizens of Bolinas, especially to the men who had hoped to secure work on the road project. The Chinese were both feared and reviled. Resentment grew, and there were grumblings across the county about the "Mongolians" up there on Bolinas Ridge.

At that time there was an organization called the California Workingmen's Party—ostensibly a political party, but also a sort of labor union for common laborers and small tradesmen of all sorts. They were vehemently anti-Chinese, and in fact opposed to anyone who hired non-white laborers. Some of the chapters even had military wings—armed militias who threatened anyone who opposed them. They had chapters in many Bay Area cities and were associated with such organizations as the Asiatic Exclusion League, the Associated Anti-Japanese Leagues, the Anti-Jap Laundry League, and the Anti-Chinese League—all organizations that we today would label as hate groups. They were extremely popular and influential. In that year of 1878 they won control of the state legislature and rewrote the state constitution.

Their leader in Marin was James S. McCue, the first white settler in Corte Madera. He had purchased land there in 1871 and raised and trained horses for a traveling circus he operated. He built a half-mile race track on his ranch near the present corner of Eastman and Buena Vista. He was also one of the founders of the Marin Water Company, the first commercial water provider in the county. Another leader was Dr. Charles C. O'Donnell of San Rafael.

The San Francisco chapter was headed by an English-born shoemaker named William Wellock. The chapter had a history of anti-immigrant violence, having organized a march that became a riot and resulted in the destruction of scores of Chinese homes and businesses and the deaths of four.

These leaders made fiery speeches to their followers, urging them to violence. On Sunday, August 4th, they held meetings to decide what to do about the "Chinese problem." They sent a letter to the Board of Supervisors, which was quoted verbatim in the *Marin County Journal*, with the original spelling:

At an Indignation meeting held at the Town Hall in San Rafael, it was mooved the following resolution be passed, wich was unanimously adopted by the meeting:

Resolved, That the Board of Supervisors has committd a groose wrong on the taxpayers of Marin county in letting the contract to build the Bollinas Road, wherby Chinemen are employed, to the exclusion of our own citizens; that it is the sence of this meeting, and we believe it to be the sence of this county, especially in view of the late election, in wich it was decided aganst the Chinemen. that Mr. Colwell, the contractor, be allowed to finish the section commenced; that he be paid for it by the county, and the ballance of the road be given to white men; that a copy of these resolutions be given to the Honorable Board of Supervisors, with the request they act on them this week, so that we can have there actions to act upon at our next meeting, on Sunday.

Signed. James Fagan.
Chairman Taxpayer's Committee.

The *Marin County Journal* attempted to quiet the situation, pointing out that the Supervisors had given the job to Colwell and Wilkins as the low bidders, without specifying what labor they would use, and thus had no say in the matter. They criticized the meeting:

Labor Excitement.
An indignation meeting was held in San Rafael last Sunday, relative to the employment of Chinese on the Bolinas road, out of which has grown some talk about forcing the Mongols to leave the work. This is sheer nonsense, and would result in nothing but trouble. The Sheriff would be bound to protect the Chinese, and he would do it. The remedy is by an arrangement with the contractors, if one can be made. They are under bonds to complete the work. We know that they will prefer to employ white labor, if they can save themselves from loss. This is the only way for the white men, who certainly ought to have the work, to accomplish their end.

Marin County Journal, 8 August 1878

But the Workingmen were having none of it. They called for a massive rally on the following Sunday:

Citizens and Taxpayers of Marin County, Rally.
THERE WILL BE A GRAND MASS Meeting of citizens, of Marin County, on SUNDAY AUGUST ELEVENTH, at 1 o'clock p.m., to take action in regard to the Board of Supervisors allowing Chinese to work on the Bolinas Road, to the exclusion of American Citizens and Taxpayers.
JOHN F. O'TOOLE,
President San Rafael W. C. P. Club.

Many residents were alarmed at the prospect of violence resulting from this rally. Fearing trouble, Sheriff James Tunstead deputized 150 armed men to ensure the rally remained peaceful.

On the day of the event Wellock, McCue, and O'Donnell came over on the morning boat from San Francisco with ten armed men. They were met by J. J. White, captain of one of the party's militias, the Shoemakers' Military Company, and the officers of one or two other "military clubs," with some ten or a dozen men from San Rafael. About noon a party of about forty men from Sausalito arrived, all heavily armed. They were preceded by an express wagon containing seventy-five Sharp's rifles, with forty rounds of ammunition for each gun. The meeting was held "on the main street" of San Rafael, probably Fourth Street at Courthouse Square.

Wellock addressed the assembly, saying they represented not just working men, but also taxpayers. They weren't seeking violence, but they objected to their taxes going to the "Celestials," a common derogatory name for Chinese. Many of the men were for riding at once up to Bolinas Ridge and "persuading" the Chinese to give up their jobs. The rally became disordered, with people shouting down any speakers who did not advocate immediate violence.

At this critical moment Sheriff Tunstead intervened, climbing onto the platform and shouting for order. He announced that the rally was an illegal assembly and threatened to arrest anyone who did not disband at once. Warily eyeing the encircled armed deputies, the rally promptly broke up. The chagrined San Francisco contingent returned to the City and held another "indignation meeting," but nothing was decided.

The following week, one of the Chinese crew was attacked when he went to Bolinas for supplies:

A brutal assault was committed on a Chinaman, at Bolinas beach, one day last week, by four white men. The Chinaman was an invalid, "infirm and old," who was boarding at the camp of the workmen on the Bolinas road. He strolled down to the beach, when these four bullies happened to pass on horseback, and they amused themselves by riding on to him, beating him unmercifully, and left him half dead. They must have been very brave and noble spirits, and when they think of it, it must appear a manly thing.

Marin County Journal, 15 August 1878

The *Journal* was pleased that worse violence was averted, but agreed that the Chinese "enemy" should not build the road:

The Practical Solution.

Messrs. Colwell & Wilkins, the contractors on the Bolinas road at San Rafael, in reply to Wellock's statement that he can furnish white men to work on the road at $1 25 a day, write as follows: "If he will furnish us with good white men who are willing to work for the same wages, or even something more than we are paying to the Chinese, with security that the white laborers will remain with us and do a day's labor for the wages, we will most cheerfully discharge the Chinese in our employ and complete the road with white labor." This is a practical remedy for the whole matter. The complaint of the white men is that their own money, paid for taxes, goes to Chinamen. And it is true, and the truth is galling, and there ought to be a remedy. Now, here it is. If there are white men out of work, who are willing to work, it is better for them to take the job, at a slight advance on the Chinese wages. By this they will accomplish the double good of getting so much money themselves, and keeping it from the enemy.

Marin County Journal, 22 August 1878

Apparently there were no takers, and the Chinese laborers built the entire road. Sheriff Tunstead's quick and decisive action very likely prevented what could have been a bloody battle with scores of heavily-armed Workingmen against 150 deputies and 16 armed white men at the camp, and the 250 unarmed Chinese in the middle. But now, with violence averted, the road construction could continue.

Crossing Bolinas Ridge

The partners were spending more money than planned, and at the end of August, they went back to the Board of Supervisors to request an advance. The Board sniffed that:

And whereas the said Colwell & Wilkins are desirous of receiving an advance upon the payments for the work now done, although neither section of said road is completed, or in such condition that it can by the Board be approved or accepted.

Road Minutes, 30 August, 1878

But they agreed to release $1,800 to cover their expenses. Two weeks later, they advanced an additional $500. At the end of September, they paid $1,650, and on October 10th, $400 more.

The *Journal* reported glowingly on the progress of the work:

The Bolinas Road

We are informed that the four sections of the Bolinas road, now being built by Colwell & Wilkins, will be practically finished by November 1st. If so, the new route can be traveled after that time, as the portion on this side of the mountain is already passable. By this route, Bolinas Bay is but sixteen miles away from San Rafael, and Burge's Hotel, on Bolinas Point, but eighteen. A gentleman who is very familiar with Tamalpais Mountain tells us that many of the finest views he has ever seen from its heights, are obtainable from the line of the new road. The drive passes through gulches of almost tropical verdure, and presents some of the most magnificent scenery to be found on the coast. The completion of this road will have far more than a local interest.

Marin County Journal, 26 September 1878

The work crews were already falling behind schedule as they laboriously hacked their way up Bolinas Ridge, but by early Fall they reached the top, completing Section Four. The work went more quickly on the generally level ridgetop.

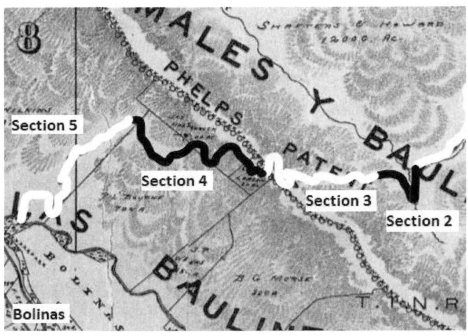

Sections 2 through 5 on a detail of Austin's 1873 Marin County map.

But now they faced Section Three, the steep descent on the north side of Bolinas Ridge. This was the most difficult portion of the entire route, with hundreds of massive redwoods and firs to be cut down and removed, and drilling and blasting nearly every foot of the way. Already two months behind schedule, they found the going agonizingly slow.

The cross-slope was so steep there was no place to stage equipment alongside the route, or even stand. Platforms had to be built for the men to stand on as they worked the rock drills to place the dynamite. It was more like tunneling than normal road building.

All materials and supplies had to be driven out from San Rafael and up the new road to the camp, an all-day drive. At sixteen feet wide, the road was too narrow for wagons to easily turn around, and a spooked horse or a wheel dropped off the edge could mean a fall of hundreds of feet. September passed, and October began. The project was supposed to be done by December 1st, but they still had miles to go.

In order to get down the steep slope, they had to build a series of switchbacks, each nearly on top of the next, forming steep hairpin turns.

Mailbox Curve. In the 1890s, there was a mailbox here for Joseph Longley's dairy on top of Bolinas Ridge. Photo by Brad Rippe. See the frontispiece for an older view of the same curve.

By the middle of October they had pushed the road down the steepest part of the ridge, completing Section Three. Now they started on Section Two, the final portion of their contract. Although this section was only a mile and a half long, it presented serious challenges. They first had to build another series of switchbacks down into Cataract Canyon. Cataract Creek is a series of scenic waterfalls that plunge a total of a thousand feet in only a little more than a mile. In the rainy season these cascades thunder and roar, their sound filling the canyon. But that autumn the canyon was rocked by the sound of blasting, sawing, and hammering as the men built a preliminary bridge between the nearly vertical walls of the canyon. On the far side, the road made a sharp left and followed the creek through thick forest down to its junction with Lagunitas Creek.

Just downstream from the creek junction was the abandoned site of Isaac Shaver's sawmill and logging settlement. From this point on, Colwell's teamsters would be able to bring supplies from San Rafael on the logging track rather than make the long journey through Olema and Bolinas.

Then they had to cross Lagunitas Creek, requiring the construction of a large bridge. The creek at this point was funneling all the water from the north side of Mount Tamalpais into the steep rocky canyon below, so it was a rushing torrent. Sturdy stone piers would have to be constructed, high enough to withstand the winter floods.

It had taken more than three months just to cross Bolinas Ridge. Colwell and Wilkins had thought they would be at this point by September, but it was now the end of October and the rains would soon set in. They realized they would need more money to build the bridge and finish Section Two. They went back to the Board of Supervisors and asked them to pay for the finished sections, though the contract had not mentioned any advances.

On October 30, the three Supervisors rode out to inspect the new road. They returned the following day:

> The Board of Supervisors having in a body passed over and fully examined Sections 3, 4, and 5 of the Bolinas Bay & Fairfax Road and being satisfied after such personal examination that the said Sections 3, 4, & 5 are finished and completed substantially in accordance with the Contract for the Construction of said Sections;
> It is ordered by the Board that said Sections 3, 4, & 5 be and are hereby accepted by the Board for and on behalf of Marin County.

Road Minutes, October 31, 1878

The Board paid the contractors the final $2,025 for those sections and the work continued. The carpenters first built a temporary bridge so they could work on both sides of the river simultaneously. With the project so far behind schedule, completing the road had to be the primary objective, and they left the building of permanent bridges till later.

Scaffolding was erected across the many side creeks and ravines to allow men and materials to be sent across.

Although Section One, the longest portion of the road, was not yet built, by making use of Isaac Shaver's existing lumber road it was now possible to drive from Ross to Bolinas. The *Journal* waxed enthusiastic:

> By the last of next week, or a very little later, you can drive to Bolinas by way of the new road. If the weather is favorable, many will drive over it this season, just for the novelty of the thing; and next year it will be such a popular drive that many will be attracted from the city and other places, to enjoy its magnificent mountain scenery, and the ocean delights at its sunset terminus.
>
> *Marin County Journal*, 14 November 1878

Three weeks later, Dr. Taliaferro (pronounced Tolliver)[14], a respected and much-loved physician from San Rafael, was determined to be the first to drive a vehicle over the new road, completed or not. It was clearly more a stunt than a pleasure drive, as the *Journal* reported December 5th, 1878:

> Dr. Taliaferro has driven over the Bolinas road the first buggy to roll over it. But he couldn't have done it if the workmen had not carried his buggy over the bridgeless chasms, sometimes swinging it across with ropes.

When the road was finished, the work crews went back and completed all the bridges. Finally, on December 19, 1878, only 18 days behind schedule, they completed Section Two, the last under the contract.

Makin Grade

The road between San Rafael and Ross was a separate project, in essence a sixth section. It was awarded to Robert G. Makin and construction ran concurrently with the Colwell-Wilkins job. Makin started his road from Laurel Grove in Ross and reached the top of

---

[14] Alfred Walker Taliaferro (1825-1885) came around the Horn in 1850 and bought one of the earliest homesteads in San Rafael. He was the first doctor at San Quentin prison and later a member of the State Assembly and Senate. He and his partner Dr. Henry Augustus DuBois (1840-1897) were the founders of Mount Tamalpais Cemetery.

Southern Heights Ridge in August 1878. This road is still known as the Makin Grade. He continued it down the steep northern slope past the San Rafael Brewery at the end of Greenwood Avenue, so this portion was called the Brewery Grade. On December 19th, the same day Colwell finished, Makin announced that he was done as well. The same day the *Journal* rhapsodized:

> The Makin grade is now finished, and affords some of the most charming views. This is the most direct route to the Bolinas road. Mr. Coleman is tracing the hills back of Magnolia Park with streets, which wander in and out and meander up the heights with such easy ascents, and lead to so many pleasant surprises of beautiful scenery, that the young and sentimental recall the stories of Fairy Land, and people the nooks and glens with houries and nymphs. Have you driven over the new Makin grade? If not, you have a treat in store. Drive due west past the brewery, right into the forest; you will think at every succeeding bend you reach that the road goes no further; but on it goes, by an easy grade, a good broad way, wide enough all the distance for two carriages. Take a gentle team, or have a driver, for your eyes will be full of beauty, and you will want to do nothing but look. The successive views of the town, the hills on the north, and the flats to the south, changing with every turn of your wheels, remind one of a revolving kaleidoscope.

On Christmas Eve, the Supervisors rode over the new roads and pronounced both projects complete. It was quite a Christmas present to the people of the county. Colwell & Wilkins received the remaining $850 on their contract. It was said they had lost $500 on the job. Even though Section One from Ross to Alpine remained to be built, it was now possible to use Shaver's old logging road to drive from San Rafael all the way to Bolinas.

The first person to actually drive the entire road was Supervisor John Charles Gibson, the man who had signed the contract to build it:

> J. C. Gibson drove over the new Bolinas road, one horse, with two in buggy, in three hours, and drove very slowly.
>
> *Marin County Journal* 26 December 1878

The *Journal* was admiring how little time it now took to get to Bolinas, but anyone who has driven the road can understand why

64

Supervisor Gibson drove slowly, especially as his was the first vehicle to cross some of those bridges.

Almost immediately, travelers started raving about the new road:

San Francisco, Jan. 15, 1879.

Ed. *Journal:* I had the good fortune to ride from San Rafael to Bolinas, in company with others from the City, over the new mountain road.

We left San Rafael on a fine morning, and made the journey in the space of three hours, without haste, as we were inclined to enjoy the mountain air and scenery, and we amused ourselves by contrasting the easy journey of the present time, with a pair of fast horses, upon a good road, with the toilsome horseback rides of other days, over the mountain trails. Doubtless many of your readers have already enjoyed the drive and are so familiar with the country that a description from my pen would afford them but little interest; but to those who have not, it would be well to suggest that one can hardly devote a day of recreation to a better purpose than this same mountain drive.

My mind was enraptured in remembrance of the little mountain streams which dash over the rocks down the ravines, and then pursue their winding course onward with the musical ripple that poets delight to write about, the majestic trees which have stood in lonely grandeur so many years, visited only by the solitary traveler or sportsman, the green hill sides with their carpet of moss and ferns, and the extended view of land and sea from the summit of the mountain, but they must be seen for an adequate idea of their beauty. On approaching Bolinas Bay there was much to attract our attention. The comfortable homes dotted here and there along the shore indicate success and comfort that are always pleasing to behold. The village presents changes all for its advantage, showing that it is by no means inert or sleepy. Three new, substantial, tastefully built churches stand in friendly proximity to each other, and there are many other evidences of moral progress such as commodious school houses, Druids hall, Temperance hall, etc. Of course we found refreshments for man and beasts at the Bay View Hotel, and did not lack for attention from the genial host and his wife, whom we found to be a very intelligent English lady.[15] We took a stroll on the old familiar beach, the same, and yet not the same, for the ocean is ever at work making imperceptible changes; and watched the surf roll in at our feet with the same fascination that it had for us years ago, and we felt that it was good for us to revisit these scenes of our early life. It has always been a source of wonder that more travelers and pleasure seekers have not found their way to that charming little seaside resort, which for its very solitude and quiet would be the more attractive to those who are anxious to escape from the turmoil and bustle of the city. And now that it offers the additional inducement of a delightful ride over the mountain from San Rafael, it is safe to predict that Bolinas will have the throng of summer visitors which it so truly deserves.

Alexis.

Marin County Journal, 23 January 1879

But with the new year came the rains—and the first of many washouts on the new road. On February 24, Judge Phinney[16] of San Rafael came over from Bolinas and reported considerable damage on the west side of the ridge, though the eastern side was still hard and smooth. William Blodgett, who had helped survey the road with Austin and who bid on the construction, was sent out and had the road repaired the same week. But the road was still incomplete.

The Last Section

So Makin's road from San Rafael to Ross was now finished, as well as Colwell and Wilkins' road from Bolinas to Alpine. But Section One, the connection between Ross and Alpine, remained to be built, and at 6¼ miles it was by far the longest. On the last day of February, 1879, the Board of Supervisors called for bids on Section One. Colwell and Wilkins wanted to do the job, but they had learned their lesson regarding Chinese laborers. On March 13th, they placed an ad in the *Journal* calling for a meeting of all contractors who intended to bid:

---

[15] George Burge (1830-1919) and his wife Emma Davis Burge (1842-bef. 1900), both English, ran the Bay View Hotel, which included a dance hall and picnic grounds. George also ran the Sausalito-Bolinas stage.

[16] Timothy Warren Phinney (1815-1906), Justice of the Peace for Bolinas.

FOR WHITE LABOR.

THE BOARD OF SUPERVISORS HAVING called for proposals for building one section of the Bolinas Road, and it being very desirable that WHITE LABOR should have the preference, the undersigned hereby invite all contractors who propose to bid for the work, to meet at the Town Hall, in San Rafael, MONDAY EVENING, March 17th at 7.30 o'clock, to agree on WHITE LABOR, as the basis of the bids.

COLWELL & WILKINS

The *Journal* thought this proposal was only fair and reasonable:

White Labor. —Colwell & Wilkins call on contractors to come together and agree on employing white labor, as the basis of their bids for the job on the Bolinas road. This will put the matter on a fair and just footing, and give the labor where all such work should be, to taxpayers and citizens.

The meeting was held and apparently all agreed. On March 28th, the three sealed bids were opened. They were:

J. Colwell	$4,475.00
J. C. Lyman	$4,650.00
W. M. Blodgett	$4,850.00

On April 16th, the Supervisors met again to select the contractor. This time they were careful to specify the labor requirements:

The Board having under consideration the construction of the Bolinas Bay & Fairfax Road, and having examined and considered the several bids presented for the construction of said Road and find Jesse Colwell the lowest bidder.

It is therefore ordered that the contract for the construction of said Section No. One of said Road be and the same is hereby awarded to said Jesse Colwell, for the sum of Four Thousand Four hundred & seventy-five dollars, upon his entering into a Contract for the Construction thereof, binding himself to construct the same and to use no Chinese or Mongolian labor and entering into bonds for the faithful performance of the said work in the sum of One Thousand Dollars, with two or more sureties to be approved by this Board.

Road Minutes, 16 April, 1878

Jesse Colwell again had the job, but this time without his partner. James Wilkins gave up contracting and began a career in journalism. That same month he founded the *Marin County Tocsin*, a rival to the *Journal*.

The next day Colwell placed an ad in the *Journal*:

Workmen Wanted.—Jesse Colwell wants 25 laborers, for work on the Bolinas Road, to commence 28th inst. No Chinese will be employed.

Meanwhile, the existing road was getting more travel as the weather improved. On May Day, the Bolinas correspondent of the *Journal* reported:

Bolinas, April 28th. Pleasure seekers have already commenced coming to this seaside resort. Four wagon loads from San Rafael were seen on the beach on Saturday, 26th inst. This was doubtless a lookout party. The time for permanent campers has scarcely come yet, the weather being still uncertain. Soon, however, we hope to see the beach lined with tents and the surf filled with bathers. The scenery about Bolinas is fine, especially over the new road, as many can testify. Nothing, we believe, (in Marin county, at least) can compare with it. At the summit of the mountain between San Rafael and Bolinas, the upper part of San Francisco bay, Tomales and Bolinas bays, and the ocean beyond the Farallone islands, about 25 miles distant, come within the range of vision. A ride of two and a half hours from San Rafael will bring you to this point. Ye admirers of the beauties of nature, come and see.

M.

Colwell apparently found enough white workers, for he and his crew started building the final section of the road from Ross in early May, 1879. They followed the existing logging track through Phoenix Gulch, and cut the steep climb of the new Shaver Grade alongside the creek up to the divide above Five Corners. They dropped down across Bontempi Ranch and made use of existing farm lanes going to the Liberty Ranch, then turned south down Lagunitas Creek to hit the end of the new road at Alpine.

Although the contract said Colwell would not be paid till the end of the job, by the end of May, he asked for and received an advance of $1,800, and on June 25th, another for $2,175. The following day, he declared the section done and invited the Board to inspect it. They found that he had not met all the specifications for the materials, but they determined that the substitutions did not compromise the road. Accordingly, they proposed, and he agreed, to reduce the overall price by $75. He was paid a final $425 and the Board declared the project completed to their satisfaction.

Finally, on June 26, 1879, after eleven months and nine days, the entire Bolinas-San Rafael Road was done—though it was called variously the Bolinas Road, the Bolinas-Fairfax Road, and the Bolinas Bay and Fairfax Road, though it didn't go to Fairfax at all. It was sixteen miles long and sixteen feet wide, and had 48 culverts and 29 bridges. It had cost $16,000 (about 23% over budget) and was immediately famed throughout the area for its magnificent views.

One very pleased taxpayer was a man we will meet again, John Oscar Eldridge (1828-1885):

Mr. J. O. Eldridge, who with Mr. Lee, visited Bolinas last week, tells us that, notwithstanding all he had read in the *Journal*, he was not prepared for the reality. He says Bolinas is the most attractive point on the California coast, and the drive from San Rafael over the new road, and return via Sausalito, is the most delightful he has ever seen in the State. Mr. Eldridge has tried them all.

Marin County Journal, 4 September 1879

In November, William Wallace Wilkins, who owned the ranch at the Bolinas end of the road, complained that his cattle were endangered by the road across his land. He put up a gate across the road and asked the Board of Supervisors to either build a fence along the road or pay him $750. They agreed to pay, and Wilkins took down his gate—and presumably built the fence himself. In May 1880, for undisclosed reasons, they awarded him another $279 and allowed him to erect across the road a self-closing gate he had invented and patented himself to keep his cattle from escaping.

The December rains again took their toll and the Old Shaver Grade got another brief life:

> Mr. Robt. Ingram tells us that the Bolinas road from Lagunitas to Bolinas is in first rate order, but along the Shaver grade, that is, this end of the road, it is so bad that travel goes by the old road, through the bed of the creek. There are no slides or impediments to cause expensive repairs, but the mud is deep.
>
> *Marin County Journal*, 18 December 1879

It must have been quite a ride in a buggy or wagon to drive up the rocky streambed. This section was still closed in January:

> The new road over the Shaver grade to Bolinas is closed, and the travel goes by the old road. The first bridge on this end has had to be secured by a rope. The road over the mountain is in splendid shape.
>
> *Marin County Journal*, 1 January 1880

This rather alarming report referred to the bridge over Ross Creek, now in Natalie Coffin Greene Park. It was quickly followed by a rather unconvincing reassurance:

> The first bridge on this end of the Bolinas road is tied with a rope, but we are informed that it is not and has not been in any danger. It is high above the flood.
>
> *Marin County Journal*, 15 January 1880

After the rains stopped, a contractor, William A. Lando of Lagunitas, was sent out to repair the road and bridge, but it was June 17th before the work was done and the road reopened. It had been closed for six months. Traffic on the road resumed and it remained a popular drive, but not without some danger:

> A huge bear crossed the Bolinas road a few days since, just in front of a buggy, and so close as to startle the horse and driver. Bruin passed on without hugging anybody, but the young couple in the buggy—well, they sat closer together, and that's all we'll tell.
>
> *Marin County Journal*, 24 June 1880

The road so many had worked to create was finally a reality. Even before the Bolinas-San Rafael road was finished, a stagecoach line was set up to make use of it.

BOLINAS ROAD NEAR SAN RAFAEL.

FAIRFAX-BOLINAS ROAD 1985: "MAILBOX CURVE"
Illustration courtesy of Dewey Livingston

The Gibson Stagecoach, 1879-1882

In June 1879, 30-year-old Henry Gibson, younger half-brother of Supervisor John Gibson, bought a flatbed wagon, fitted it with three bench seats and a canvas canopy, and on August 28th advertised the business (though the *Journal* used his brother's name by mistake):

Henry Brown Gibson was born in Iowa in 1849 and lived there until at least 1870. By 1875 he was living in Bolinas, and in June 1877 he married Adeline Florenda Sebrean (1850-1913). She was the daughter of Francisco Sebrean and

Bolinas Stage Line.

ON AND AFTER MONDAY, September 15, 1879, the San Rafael and Bolinas Stage Line will make TRI-WEEKLY TRIPS, leaving BOLINAS Monday, Wednesday and Friday, and connecting with the 11 A.M. train for the city; and leaving San Rafael Tuesday, Thursday and Saturday, at 12 o'clock noon.

The undersigned has bought the whole route, and will spare no pains to make it in every way agreeable to his patrons.   J. C. GIBSON.

Maria Jésus Briones, daughter of Gregorio Briones, the patriarch of Bolinas. The Gibsons had three children, but all of them died within a five year span.

Gibson based his Bolinas Stage Line at the Marin Stables on the south side of Fourth Street, just across from the courthouse. The stage would be hitched to its four-horse team, then driven down to the railroad station to take on passengers, many of whom had arrived by train from Sausalito or Fairfax. Once loaded, the stages would head west down Fourth Street, then turn left on D, the main road heading south out of town.

The Bolinas Stage Line started business as soon as the road was finished. The stage soon began carrying the mail, making it an even more important part of the community. The trip took three hours and cost a dollar and a half, the equivalent of almost $35 today. San Francisco residents on holiday could now catch the early ferry to

Sausalito and the train to San Rafael, and the stage could get them to Bolinas in time for a late lunch.

The Bolinas Stage in front of the Central Hotel on Fourth Street in San Rafael. Wallace Sayers driving. From the Ted Wurm / Fred Runner collection.

Conditions could be rugged. In the wet season parts of the road became a mass of mud; washouts and landslides were common. In dry weather the mud dried into iron-hard ruts and the dust was terrible. Women often wore veils over their faces and both men and women wore long coats called dusters to protect their clothes. Spring-fed drinking troughs were maintained at several points along steeper stretches of the road. Often hunters or hikers would ask the driver to let them off at some likely spot and pick them up on the way back. On one occasion the passengers had to share their seats with a 221-pound bear two of the men had shot. Another time two young women were picking huckleberries for a picnic near Bolinas and encountered a bear bent on the same task. One of the women, a crack shot, killed the bear and they brought the carcass to San Rafael in the stage. Picnickers were tough in those days.

The Bolinas coaches didn't look like movie stagecoaches. They were open wagons with three wooden seats and a canvas roof that could be rolled back on fine days. Six passengers faced forward and three back.

The driver sat on a high seat in front. If you were friends with the driver—or a pretty girl—you got to ride up there beside him. A leather boot in back held luggage, light freight, guns, and fishing rods. The coaches were pulled by teams of four strong draft horses and driven by some colorful characters.

A good stagecoach driver was envied by men and admired by women. He sat up there on the high seat with a cigarette dangling from a lip, the "ribbons"[17] and a rawhide whip held casually in special calfskin driving gloves. Quick runs were expected, and the drivers had to judge the curves and road conditions carefully. The steel tires would skitter to the very edge on the many sharp hairpin turns. It was not a ride for the faint of heart, but the drivers were skilled and experienced and the line had an excellent safety record. Many of these drivers became prominent citizens.

One driver, Robert Cottingham, assisted the victims of an alarming accident between Summit and Alpine:

A Miraculous Escape.—Last Saturday, Mr. L. Gordon was driving from Bolinas to San Rafael, having with him a little daughter of his partner, Mr. Hugh Munroe, and when crossing the bridge over the first gulch this side of the mountain, his horse shied off the bridge, and plunged with the buggy and its occupants down about twenty feet on the rocks and stumps below. Miss Munroe was eased in her fall by striking in the limbs of a tree, which saved her from injury; Mr. Gordon escaped with a slight scalp wound. But the most wonderful part of it is that the horse and buggy were uninjured. R. T. Cottingham in his stage, with the band which had played the night before at the ball in Bolinas, and a gentleman in a buggy came up a few moments after the accident, and assisted in setting things to rights. The horse was tightly wedged between stumps of trees, the buggy capsized, and partly suspended by branches. The outfit as it lay there did not look to be worth five dollars. Yet when all were hauled up the bank and straightened out on the road there was found to be no damage done. It was certainly one of the most remarkable escapes ever recorded.

Marin County Journal, 12 May 1881

---

[17] Ribbons are the reins of a team.

Liberty Ranch

Vincent and Mary Jane Liberty's dairy ranch lay at about the halfway point between San Rafael and Bolinas. The stage ran right past their front gate. They started selling lunches to the passengers when the stages stopped for water. Mary Jane was a good cook and the word got around. The city people enjoyed the hearty ranch food while admiring the beautiful views of the mountain and the ridges covered with grasslands and forests on all sides.

So many expressed the desire to stay there and explore the area that Vincent and Mary Jane decided to turn the ranch into a resort. They built a number of cabins beneath the big trees. They called their new resort Liberty Ranch and it became a destination of its own. People would rent one of the cabins and spend a week hunting, hiking and riding in the hills or fishing in Lagunitas Creek. It became very popular, as shown by this article from a few years later:

Liberty's.—One of the pleasantest resorts in this neighborhood is Liberty's ranch on the road to Bolinas. Situated beside the Lagunitas stream, in a charming spot on the mountain, with the purest air and water, with trout fishing, deer, quail and rabbit shooting, in their season, and a good table supplied with abundance of fresh milk, it is no wonder that it is a favorite spot with city people who wish to rest and enjoy an outdoor life without the restrictions in dress and the late hours and dissipation inseparable from hotel life.

Marin County Journal, 8 October 1885

They soon had a major disaster. On August 18, 1881, the *Journal* reported:

Liberty Burned Out.

Wednesday last week the mountain home of Mr. Vincent Liberty, seven miles from San Rafael on the road to Bolinas, was destroyed by fire. The origin of the fire is unknown, but as it started in the girl's[18] room, soon after she had left it, it is supposed it must have been from the accidental ignition of matches. The fire spread so rapidly that very little was saved. From the house a couple of mattresses, a little bedding, and a sewing

---

[18] Elodia Josephine Liberty (1867-1954). She was fourteen at the time.

machine were rescued. Clothing, furniture, household utensils, watch, money, provisions, everything went. The barn caught fire, and Liberty only saved his horses by bursting the side out. He managed to save his spring wagon, but the heavy wagon, harness, saddles, etc., were burned. A lot of hay and grain which had just been laid in were lost. The cattle in the corral were saved by breaking the fence. A policy of insurance for $1,259 in the Southern California [Insurance Company] was in the house, but whether it did not wait till the next day to take effect—the fire was September 30th—Mr. Liberty does not know. The loss is a great misfortune to Liberty, and we shall guess wrong if the sympathy of his many friends does not take some substantial shape. His house was a favorite resort for a great many city people, and he is as widely known and liked as any man in the county.

The Libertys soon rebuilt and resumed trade. The following year, Vincent came to the aid of Henry Gibson. On March 16th, 1882, the *Journal* reported:

Mr. Gibson was delayed on his Bolinas stage last Friday. One of his horses was attacked with blind staggers[19], and fell, throwing the stage off a steep bank. Mr. Liberty helped to right the coach, and furnished a horse to come on.

After only three years of operation, in October 1882 Gibson sold the line to Robert Cottingham and opened a butcher shop at Bolinas. He was later appointed postmaster of Bolinas. By 1888 Gibson had moved to Sonoma, and in 1892 he was in Humboldt County. His wife Adeline died in 1913 and he died in 1934, aged 85.

Meanwhile, two major extensions were being made to the road.

---

[19] A disease caused by the horse eating grain contaminated with the fungus *Fusarium moniliforme*.

The Eldridge Grade, 1884

John Oscar Eldridge was born in Manhattan in 1828 and became an auctioneer. He was 20 when the gold rush began, and he joined a group of 21 adventurers to form the West Coast Trading and Mining Company. They bought the barque *St. Mary*, loaded it with mining equipment and supplies, and sailed it around Cape Horn to San Francisco, arriving September 25, 1849, after seven months and one grounding. John Eldridge soon established himself as one of the leading auctioneers in the region.

In 1856 he married Elizabeth Risdon (1830-1879),

John Oscar Eldridge (1828-1885) in the 1850s; ambrotype courtesy of his great-great-granddaughter Margo Merck.

a teacher, who gave him two daughters, Dolly and Grace. Grace later married Sydney B. Cushing, founder of the Mount Tamalpais Scenic Railway. In 1883 Eldridge and his brother-in-law founded the San Rafael Gas Company. He also dabbled in real estate. When Elizabeth died in 1879, he moved his family to San Rafael and built a mansion on the northeast corner of Fourth and Court Streets, across from the courthouse.

In November of 1882, Eldridge, known locally as Uncle Joe, proposed a road to the summit of Mount Tamalpais. The beloved mountain dominated views from many points in Marin, but it was accessible only by steep trails. Eldridge wanted a good, well-built road, easily drivable in a wagon or buggy. He said that it would not only provide recreation for locals, but would draw visitors to Marin.

He started advertising in the paper, talking up the project and soliciting subscriptions. It took some time to raise the money and public support, but by July 1884 they had raised $4,000 in pledges and decided to move forward. A preliminary meeting was held at Eldridge's home, attended by a number of prominent and wealthy men, including "Professor" Hiram Austin.

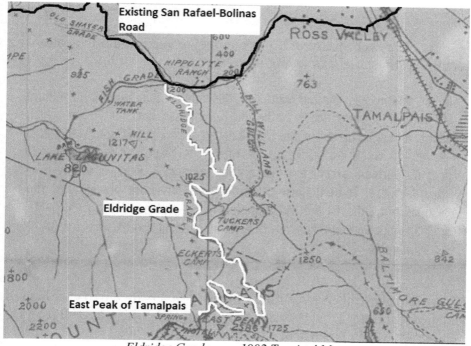

Eldridge Grade on a 1902 Tourists' Map.

Eldridge suggested that the new road branch off from the Bolinas-San Rafael Road at the foot of Fish Gulch and head due south up the north face of the mountain. Austin strongly supported the project and offered to conduct the survey. Hansen & Lund, builders, volunteered to construct a viewing platform on the mountaintop "12 to 15 feet high, to be substantial, and hold 30 to 50 people, similar to the observatories on many of the high peaks in Switzerland." San Francisco glassmaker Carlton Newman offered to donate a telescope to be installed at the summit for the use of visitors. Said Eldridge:

Think of it! A view 3,000 feet high within an hour of Frisco. A signal station on top, seven fine plateaus to stop on and turn round, if you don't want to go up the mountain. Professor Austin has studied this road for years, and says it will be the handsomest drive in America, and will beat the far-famed Dutch Flat drive, and the mountain road to Virginia City higher than a kite. Whew! Who wouldn't live in San Rafael? Let's have that drive!

J. O. Eldridge.
Marin County Journal, 24 July 1884

His pleas were answered, more money came in, and the following month Austin started surveying the new road:

Prof. Austin has started work on the road to the summit of Mount Tamalpais. It commences at the old Fish grade, the sharp pitch which leads to Lagunitas from the Bolinas road, and bearing south and east leaves the Water Co.'s lake on the right. The grade will not exceed one foot in fourteen, except in a few trifling instances, which is a very easy mountain rise. To distinguish this from the Bolinas and other roads, and also as a tribute to the indomitable energy and push with which Mr. Eldridge has worked this enterprise, it has been named the Eldridge Grade up Tamalpais.

Marin County Journal, 14 August 1884

In mid-September, one of the Chinese workers on the road collapsed and died. Coroner Eden determined the cause of death was epilepsy. By September Austin had reached the summit:

Prof. Austin finished the trail to the summit of Tamalpais this week and a large force of graders are now at work constructing the wagon road. Within thirty days it will be completed. The route takes in all the beauties of the grand mountain. Neither the pen of the poet nor the brush of the painter can do the subject adequate justice. — *San Rafael Tocsin.*[20]

---

[20] As reported in the *Daily Alta California*, 24 September 1884. They should have said *Marin County Tocsin* of San Rafael.

There were major storms in October, delaying the work as the road approached the summit. In November the consortium ran out of money and the labor contractor, Paul Trommlitz of San Francisco, pulled out of the job. Eldridge and his supporters again appealed to the public for money, saying the job was only ten days from completion. Apparently the money was raised and a new contractor found, because the road was completed on December 13, 1884. Two wagonloads of officials drove up the mountain, marveling at the views. At the summit a celebration ensued, with speeches, patriotic songs, and high-blown rhetoric:

The Eldridge Grade.
On the Brow of Old Tamalpais in a Buggy.
THE COMMITTEE AND CITIZENS INSPECT THE GRAND GRADE.
MAGNIFICENT VIEWS—LIKEWISE SPEECHES.

We are more than pleased to announce to the public that the formal opening of the Carriage Road—the Eldridge Grade—to the summit of Tamalpais Mountain, took place on Saturday last, the 13th instant, and was celebrated in a manner becoming such an auspicious event in the annals of Marin County, and, we might add, in the State of California.

We have a fair view of the road traveled, and we look down upon coil after coil of this civilized anaconda which has at last fastened itself around the rough body of the solid mountain and made it succumb to the wants and pleasure of man. We are now on the summit stretch, and have but a few hundred feet to make it. Between these points we ran upon a gang of Chinamen under the immediate command of Jas. Watson, an old veteran of the late war, blasting and rounding up the last section of the road, which had been left by the contractor unfinished. We are now standing upon the summit of Mt. Tamalpais, 3,000 feet above the level of the sea, awe-stricken and bewildered at the scene before us. Yonder away to the north is dimly seen the snow-capped Shasta. To the eastward can be seen, stretching along and far up against the blue sky, the sunny peaks of the Sierra Nevadas, while starting at their base and running south to the Coast Range, are the Sacramento, San Joaquin, Sonoma and Napa valleys, dotted over with live oaks and forests of fruit trees, farmhouses, villages and vineyards, and networked by railroads, while through the whole flows the Sacramento, San Joaquin and Russian rivers, mingling their waters in the great Bay of San Francisco. Yonder to the south, in wonderful majesty and sublimity, the restless though not boisterous Pacific, while riding upon its bosom are the "white-winged" messengers of peace and commerce, passing to and fro through the Golden Gate, laden with products of the Occident and the rich fabrics of the Orient. Beneath us the beautiful bay of Frisco, with its islands and fortifications. San Francisco, too, with its spires, domes and minarets, gilded by the rays of the noonday sun can be seen, girdled by a forest of masts carrying the ensigns of all nations.

Marin County Journal, 18 December 1884

For all its flowery enthusiasm (and it went on for several more columns), this account contains several inaccuracies. Before it was graded off for the Mill Valley Air Force base in 1950, West Peak was the highest of the three summits of Tamalpais, and it stood 2604 feet high, not 3000. Also, Mount Shasta, 237 miles away, could never be seen from the summit; the Russian River does not flow into San Francisco Bay; and there are few if any minarets in San Francisco. Oh, and it is *never* called "Frisco."

But anyone who has stood on the summit can forgive the writer's hyperbole, and on a clear winter's day the Sierra Nevada are still occasionally visible 150 miles away.

A cart on Eldridge Grade, from In Tamal Land, *by Helen Bingham, 1906.*

In February, Eldridge was still advertising for money to complete the road. The viewing platform and telescope were installed in March and the project was finally completed, accomplished entirely by private funds.

Woman at the "Locator" telescope on the East Peak of Tamalpais. Photo from the Nancy Skinner Collection, courtesy of the Lucretia Little History Room, Mill Valley Public Library.

Two weeks later, "Uncle Joe" Eldridge died unexpectedly in his sleep of an aneurism, aged only 56. The *Journal* mourned:

The town is lonesome without him. San Francisco will miss him, California will feel his loss. The news of his death was like the fall of a mighty redwood in the quiet of midnight. It stilled the hearts of men. All felt that a calamity had overtaken the community. None could realize that it could be true.

"Ay, turn and weep--'tis manliness
To be heart-broken here—
For the grave of earth's best nobleness

Is water'd by the tear."[21]

His life, while remarkable in no single, great achievement, was beautiful in that as a whole it was so well rounded and successful. His last work will be an enduring monument to his memory, and is a grand and fitting memento of his life. From the valley his eye was ever on the mountaintop, and whatever the difficulties, each day's journey brought him nearer the summit. Alas, he has gone; and in the death of J. O. Eldridge every man has lost a friend!

Marin County Journal, 5 March 1884

The Eldridge Grade immediately became a very popular route for hikers, bicyclists, and drivers. It is frequently mentioned in the hiking guides of the time and the many newspaper articles extolling the beauties of the mountain. One Sunday that May, more than a hundred people went up the Eldridge Grade in buggies, carriages, on horseback, on bicycle and on foot. The *Journal* suggested that an enterprising man should build an inn at the summit with refreshments for travelers.

Unfortunately, winter storms closed the road almost every winter, and each year there would be another subscription to pay for repairs. After a particularly damaging series of storms in 1891, Roadmaster LeCornec[22] repaired the road yet again, and appealed to the Board of Supervisors to accept the grade as a public road. They did not agree, no doubt aware of the frequent maintenance costs. It washed out again in January 1892 and W. H. Jewell undertook repairs. When it washed out again in April 1892, it remained closed for two years, though that did not stop some hikers:

A pedestrian party of seventeen ladies and gentlemen and little folks, went up the Eldridge grade Saturday to the top of Mount Tamalpais. There were some from San Francisco and Oakland, and Wm. Sale and family and Mrs. Clifford and family of San Rafael in the party. The road is so damaged by the season's storms as to be impassable in one place near the foot of the grade, but this was overcome by the use of saplings.

---

[21] The poem is by Nathaniel Parker Willis (1806-1867).
[22] Roadmasters were publicly-appointed officials charged with monitoring and repairing roads. Peter LeCornec (1833-1908), a native of France, settled at Ross Landing.

The road is rough and rocky at other points, but Mr. Sale estimates that to put it in good order would not cost more than $100. The trip was one of hearty enjoyment, though the ladies walked every foot of the way. The day was exceptionally clear and beautiful. By the way, we have heard that James McCue will run a line of carriages to the summit this summer, and we hope this is true. There is no mountain trip on the coast so easy of access and so full of interest as this.[23]

Marin Journal[24], 12 April 1894

Hiking, running, and bicycling clubs became very popular and there were frequent outings and competitions. In 1892, the Gentlemen's Cross-County Club announced a challenge by one of their "wheelmen":

Several members of the club ride bicycles, and one of the wheelmen has issued a challenge to the pedestrians to race him from Sausalito via Mill Valley and the summit of Mount Tamalpais, thence to Larsen's Inn and then to Camp Taylor. The country to be traversed is steep and rocky in many places, while in others the brush and ferns are so dense as to be almost impassable, and it will be necessary to carry the wheel overhead for a considerable distance. The rider in question rides an "ordinary,"[25] never has used a "safety," and proposes the contest to demonstrate that the "ordinary," backed by pluck and endurance will "go" places where many men would fail to get through on foot even with the assistance of hill-climbing shoes and alpenstocks.

San Francisco Call, 27 May 1892

The Grade was further damaged in March of 1895, and the *Journal* urged its readers to step up and foot the bill for repairs, lest the road be "left in ruins." It was repaired that summer and in use again by June. But in 1896 the Scenic Railway was built up the south side of the mountain and Tamalpais Tavern was built near the summit of East Peak. The Eldridge Grade saw much less vehicular use and fell into disrepair.

---

[23] McCue was one of the leaders of the Workingman's Party that tried to drive the Chinese off the road job.

[24] In 1888, the *Marin County Journal* changed its name to the *Marin Journal*.

[25] An ordinary bicycle has one huge front wheel and a small back wheel, later replaced by the safety bicycle with equal-sized wheels. Today's mountain bikers might find the trails a challenge on one of these antique bikes.

It was eventually closed to vehicles, though it remains a popular hiking and biking route to this day, as well as a fire road.

The Eldridge Grade was a triumph of engineering. It is 5.8 miles long, climbs over 2,000 feet, and has an average grade of 7%, though in places it is 14%, a very difficult grade for a buggy (or an aged writer). It continues to wash out most winters, and as of this writing (March 2017) is again closed. Still, it offers the easiest approach to the summit from the north, and still provides spectacular views. Uncle Joe would be proud.

John Eldridge's accomplishment in almost single-handedly organizing this project is a credit to his vision and perseverance, and he deserves to be more recognized today.

The Fairfax Grade, 1884

The other major extension of the Bolinas-San Rafael Road was the Fairfax Grade. Back in February 1884, the supervisors had voted to build the Fairfax arm of the road as requested in the initial petition of 1877. This would allow hikers and bicyclists to ride the train to Fairfax, and then have a shorter and easier trip to the backcountry. It would also provide a faster drive for those going to Liberty Ranch or the various camps and hunting clubs in the Lagunitas Valley.

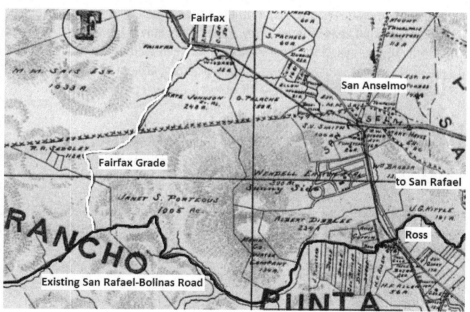

Fairfax Grade on the 1892 George Dodge map of Marin.

In June the Supervisors called for bids but apparently did not receive any, as they extended the deadline to the end of July. Finally Hiram Austin, who by now was a Supervisor himself, said that he could do the job more quickly and at a quarter the cost. The Supervisors withdrew the call for bids and on August 7 authorized Austin to build the road, the cost not to exceed $2,500. He started the job immediately, simultaneously with the Eldridge Grade. He contracted with a Mr. Riley to grade the road and work started on August 4, 1884.

By September 25, the *Journal* reported that both projects were progressing well:

> Mr. Austin is progressing rapidly with the Fairfax road, and expects to have it completed by the first of November. It will be a favorite short drive around from Fairfax to the Anselmo, and with the completion of the magnificent Eldridge grade, will fully equip the east suburbs for lovers of the road.

The grading was finished by the middle of October:

> The grading on the new Fairfax and Bolinas road is finished. Mr. Riley, who ran the grade, was not blind to the esthetic features of the beautiful drive. He found beds of ferns of royal size and symmetry. He also opened a spring by the wayside which furnished his men with excellent water in great abundance, and for which Schneider is preparing a box, to put it in shape for a permanent watering place.
>
> *Marin County Journal*, 16 October 1884

The Fairfax Grade was completed in November 1884, just a month before the Eldridge Grade. It was 2.8 miles long and had some very steep stretches as it climbed out of San Anselmo Canyon to Bon Tempe.

With the completion of the Eldridge Grade and the Fairfax Grade, the Bolinas Road and its extensions totaled 25 miles and it was once again believed to be complete. But as we shall see, it was to undergo many more changes.

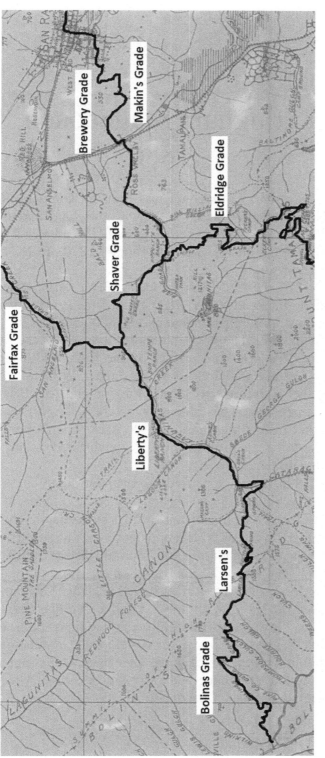

The completed road as of 1884, on the 1902 Tourists' Map

The Cottingham Stagecoach, 1882-1886

Robert Townsend Cottingham was born in Kentucky in 1832 and came to Marin soon after the Civil War. Cottingham started doing road work in 1868 and the next year was appointed Roadmaster in District 1 of the county, though he resigned in February 1870. In 1871 he became the County Assessor.

In May 1874, he bought from George Burge the stage line from Sausalito to Bolinas and started carrying the mail to Bolinas. He made a trip to the East to purchase some excellent horses and in June opened the line to the public. The stage left Sausalito every Tuesday, Thursday, and Saturday, just after the arrival of the 8:45 AM boat from San Francisco. The stage went to Easkoot Beach and Willow Camp (Stinson Beach), but the road between Bolinas Lagoon and the cliffs at the base of Mount Tamalpais was passable only at very low tides. Consequently, passengers and freight were delivered to McKennan's Landing, where Bill McKennan met them in his power launch for the short ride across the lagoon to Bolinas.

In May 1875, the Post Office Department annulled Cottingham's mail contract, sending the mail instead by rail to Olema, where it was transferred to John Nelson's Olema-Bolinas stagecoach. This must have cut into Cottingham's profits. But apparently he was doing well, because he had a new stagecoach built in 1877 and in 1881 he built a large stable in Bolinas opposite the Bay View Hotel on the shore of the lagoon. By 1881 he was driving the San Rafael stage for Henry Gibson.

In October 1882, he bought the San Rafael-Bolinas Stage Line from Gibson. Since he was now running two stage lines, he hired a second driver, Frank Page, both of whom developed a reputation for being skillful, reliable drivers. Frank Page later became a congressman, and both men credited their experience driving the stage with developing their character and sense of responsibility.

In March 1884, a severe winter storm struck the county:

> The hardest storm of the season visited us last Saturday and Sunday. The wind blew very strong, though we hear of little damage beyond the uprooting of a few trees. Cottingham had to clear the way for his Bolinas stage with an ax on Monday, and he reports a few washouts on the road. Mr. Liberty was promptly on hand, repairing the worst one.
>
> *Marin County Journal*, 13 March 1884

In 1885, Cottingham was soliciting $500 subscriptions for a project to run a telephone line to Bolinas. In December 1877, the water company had installed the first commercial telephone in the county, connecting their office in San Rafael to the dam keeper's house at Lagunitas Lake[26]. Cottingham's plan was to connect this line to Bolinas. He was apparently successful:

> Bolinas had a merry time with her telephone last Sunday. About one hundred people, old and young, men, women and children, availed themselves of the company's invitation to use the line without cost. It is a matter of great satisfaction to Bolinas, so long left one side in the march of improvements, to be connected with the world by the human voice, and it is likely that the company will be liberally patronized, while the community will be greatly benefitted.
>
> *Marin Journal*, 25 June 1885

Cottingham was also active in Democratic politics and ran for Sheriff, though he did not win the party's nomination. He was appointed to the executive committee at the state Democratic convention.

He continued to drive the coach three days a week, not without incident:

> A bear disputed the road with Bob Cottingham, driver of the Bolinas stage, last Thursday, but finally gave way gracefully and no damage resulted. Bob was not "heeled."

---

[26] This was actually the second phone line in Marin. The first, and the earliest in California, was strung between the house and dairy barn on the ranch of Adolph Mailliard near White's Hill on October 6, 1877. Alexander Graham Bell was a close friend of Mailliard and his wife and often stayed with them. Bell used the top wire of a fence for the line.

In 1886, he hired another driver, 28-year-old Leonard Nott. In September, the new man had a bad experience:

Runaway Stage.

The Bolinas stage of Monday brought as passengers Mr. and Mrs. McCrea of San Francisco, Leonard Nott driving. Mr. McCrea got out at the telegraph office, and stopping at the post office, Nott ran in with the mail. As he reached the sidewalk after leaving the mail, the team started. Leonard sprang to their heads and caught both horses near the bit, but they were too furiously started for him to stop them, and the result was that he lost his footing, and was dragged between them by the bits. The team turned on to the sidewalk at Cheda's office, where the stage collided with the building, and Nott lost his hold. By this time Mrs. McCrea, with great presence of mind, had reached forward and taken the reins, and pulled so hard on them that she skinned her hands. The team followed the sidewalk until the stage collided with a big tree which stands nearly in the center. Here the horses cleared from the stage, the whippletrees giving away. Mrs. McCrea kept her seat, and escaped unhurt, though not a little frightened, as well she might be. Poor Nott was taken into Cheda's office, in an unconscious state. The doctor says that no bones were broken, though the stage probably passed over his thigh, and he had some concussion of the brain.

Later.

It is now found that he received no internal injuries, and will probably soon be out again. It was a wonderful escape both for Mrs. McCrea and Nott, and both displayed true heroism.

Marin County Journal, 30 September 1886

His employer must have been satisfied with his young driver's performance, because two months later Cottingham sold the line to Nott.

Cottingham later became County Treasurer. The next year he purchased a drug store in Tomales. He died in San Rafael in 1909, aged 77.

The Nott Stagecoach, 1886-1890

Leonard Nott was born in Bolinas in February 1858. He was one of nine children of Hiram Nott (1826-1870) and Maria Rosita Briones (1833-1901), another daughter of Gregorio Briones.

By the time he was 21 in 1879, he was driving the Sausalito-Bolinas stage for Bob Cottingham. Seven years later, in November 1886, he bought the business. The following January he married Carolyn D. Lauff (1867-1956), daughter of Charles Augustus Lauff (1822-1917), one of the first American pioneers in Bolinas[27].

That driving a stage could be dangerous was brought home to all on Christmas day of 1879. James Steele, 41, a driver on the Sausalito to Bolinas line, was thrown from his seat by the rough road. He became entangled in the reins and was dragged feet-first to his death.[28]

On March 8th, 1889, the *Sausalito News* published a glowing report about Bolinas and the stage line:

A representative of the *Sausalito News* made a special trip by private conveyance for the purpose of looking at this far-famed and popular little town on the Ocean's shore, where the waters of the great Pacific rise and fall. There are two direct ways of reaching Bolinas from the North Pacific Coast railroad; one by the way of San Rafael and Ross station to Fairfax, up the heavy grade to the summit of the Tamalpais ridge, through a most beautiful and picturesque country. The highest elevation reached by this route is about 1,500 feet above the sea level. The grade is a rise of one foot in fourteen most of the way to the summit and consequently quite gradual. A splendid and extensive view of the ocean and coast shore is commanded on the Bolinas side of the ridge.

The San Rafael and Bolinas Mail Stage Line makes three trips a week each way, laying over at Bolinas Sunday and making the first trip

---

[27] See *Reminiscences of Charles Lauff,* by the author, 2016.
[28] *Daily Alta California*, 25 December 1887.

from there Monday, returning the next day, and so on through the week. This Stage Line is one [of] the best equipped on the Coast, and conveys the bulk of the travel from the Narrow Gauge railroad to Bolinas. Three stages are run in summer when the travel is heavy. But the horses are what took our eye. They are most magnificent specimens of the animal kingdom and it is safe to say no stage line in the country can surpass them in beauty or speed. The Line is owned by Mr. Leonard Knott [sic], who is widely known as a very skillful stage driver, and he never spares any pains or trouble to make his passengers comfortable. The stage line over this route was started in 1874, by one of the veterans of Marin County, Mr. R. T. Cottingham, who ran it successfully for ten years.[29]

In 1879, James M. Donahue completed his San Francisco & North Pacific Railroad from San Rafael to Petaluma. This eliminated the need for the stage line between those cities, as the 1870 San Rafael & San Quentin Railroad had killed that stage line, and the 1874 North Pacific Coast Railroad did in the stage between San Rafael and Sausalito. Old-timers missed the many stagecoaches rattling through town:

San Rafael has but one stage line, and that runs to Bolinas. When Nott's four-in-hand bowls gaily through the town, it carries us back to the good old times when travel was nearly all done by stage, and slugs were as common as dollars are now.

Marin Journal, 4 July 1889

The Longleys

Thomas Longley (1805-1882) came to San Francisco in a wagon train in 1857. His wife Mary died on the trail, leaving his 23-year-old daughter Sarah to care for her brother Charles, 5. The family moved to Olema the following year and Sarah married David Olds, who had a ranch at Five Brooks. Thomas operated a dairy on the Olds ranch. In 1865 Thomas and Charles moved up to a remote site on Bolinas Ridge, where they built a two-story house. Thomas died, leaving his estate to Charles, then 18. In 1886 Charles married Emma Brunotte (1862-1949),

---

[29] The *News* was confused in its last statement. Cottingham bought the Sausalito-Bolinas Stage in 1874 and the San Rafael-Bolinas Stage in 1882, and he only ran it four years. Also, the line was started by Henry Gibson, not Robert Cottingham.

and two years later they sold the home place and bought a tract of land on Bolinas Ridge, just east of Summit House, where they built a cabin. To receive their mail, they built a trail down to one of the switchbacks on the Bolinas-Fairfax Road and carved a mailbox out of a massive redwood. The San Rafael stage would drop off their mail as it passed. The Longleys became friends of the Libertys; Mary Jane Liberty helped to deliver their son Louis (1888-1964) at the cabin on the ridge. They built a barn and a cooler shed, planted an orchard, and ran twenty dairy cattle. But a severe snowstorm and disease wiped out the herd in 1890 and they lost a baby boy. Wiped out, they moved to Woodville, now Dogtown. Though their stay on the ridge was brief, their orchard and their mailbox still stands.

On busy summer days people flocked to the beach for holidays at the Bolinas hotels and Captain Easkoot's Willow Camp. These camps were very popular, with groups of twenty or thirty spending a week or more together, swimming, sunbathing, hiking, fishing, and hunting[30]. On very busy days, Leonard Nott put on more stages:

Three stages and twenty-eight passengers was Nott's measure from Bolinas Monday morning, and still the woods over there are full of them.

Marin County Journal, 28 July 1887

The stagecoach ride was a memorable event for many passengers. In 1974, 91-year-old Mabel Bullis reminisced about the trip, made around 1889 when she was six:

We boarded the stage that carried the mail and passengers from San Rafael to Bolinas every day. The route was up the old Fairfax Grade, then a long, slow climb up the Bolinas Ridge, until the summit was reached. That was a thrilling moment, when the whole world seemed suddenly spread out before us, and the four horses began to trot down the hill, swinging us around the sharp curves at fully twelve miles an hour!

Early Bolinas Memories, by Mabel Dodge Bullis

---

[30] The hunting brought risks. That October when deer season opened, an over-eager camper accidentally shot the camp proprietor (and former County Surveyor) Alfred Easkoot. He was severely wounded but survived. *Sacramento Daily Union*, 15 October 1877.

95

In July 1889 there was another case of a runaway horse on the Bolinas-Fairfax:

Frightful Runaway.—Last Saturday Mr. Chas. S. Barney was driving to Bolinas. Descending the grade on the Bolinas side of the mountain, his horse stumbled and fell to his knees. He recovered himself, but almost immediately stumbled again, this time falling completely, and breaking a thill and the whiffletree[31]. Mr. Barney was thrown out, and went so far down the bank that he had only the end of the reins in his hands, and the buggy striking the horse's heels, he pulled away, and flew down the hill driverless. Fortunately no team was coming up the grade, to take the awful chances of meeting a runaway horse and buggy. Mr. Robert Strain and another gentleman were going down the grade in a family wagon with a span[32]. Mr. Strain took the best position he could to receive the shock. The horse struck his wagon, and then went past him, at that point becoming detached from the buggy, which went down the bank about 200 feet. The horse stopped at the gate, and when Mr. Barney reached him he was quietly grazing in the field. Neither the horse nor buggy was very much injured. A curious thing was that at one point on the road all the contents of the buggy—boxes of fruit, melon, papers, bottles of medicine, etc.—were deposited together, and yet the buggy appeared not to have been capsized, and there were no marks on the road to indicate an upset. How the horse could make that flying descent, and get around the sharp turns, without striking the bank with the buggy, or slewing it off the road, is among the miracles of runaway accidents. But it was done. A very few moments before the accident occurred, Mr. Barney met on the grade the writer of this, with three young folks in his carriage. If we had been a little later, and met the horse without a driver, flying down upon us with the buggy swaying—well, we don't know what then, and are very glad we don't.

Marin Journal, 25 July 1889

---

[31] A thill is the shaft extending from the front of the wagon and a whiffletree is the cross-piece to which the horses are harnessed.

[32] A two-horse team.

Summit House

Larsen's Summit House. Courtesy Jack Mason Museum of West Marin History.

Seeing the success of Liberty's resort, Christian Frederick Larsen thought to establish another stagecoach stop along the road. Little is known about Larsen. He was born around 1836 in Denmark, so would have been in his fifties at this time. He had done occasional work as a road laborer for the county; perhaps he had even helped to build the road.

In 1887, he bought 20 acres of land at the very summit of Bolinas Ridge (now at the intersection of the Bolinas-Fairfax and Ridgecrest Boulevard).

In the redwood grove on the north side of the road he built a rustic log cabin inn with wide verandas. He located a good spring a few hundred yards to the east and installed a Diesel engine and a pump to send the water across the road to his inn. He opened his resort in 1888 as Summit House. Almost immediately he was sued by Pablo Briones for selling liquor without a license. Larsen appealed to the Board of Supervisors:

Mr. Larson [sic], of the Ridge on the Bolinas road, appeared before the Board and asked that the proceedings commenced against him for selling liquor without a license be dismissed, as he was not guilty of the charge, and that the whole thing was a conspiracy of enemies to do him an injustice. Consideration postponed to allow thorough investigation.

Sausalito News, 25 January 1889

Larsen must have prevailed, because on February 28, the Board granted him a liquor license.

In October 1890 a fire broke out just north of Bolinas in Woodville (now Dogtown) and the flames soon spread up the steep slopes of Bolinas Ridge, burning the Wilkins ranch (and his patented self-closing gate) and several others.

Descending the road with a load of passengers from San Rafael, Nott found himself confronting a wall of flame. Said the *Journal* on October 30:

Summit House,

BOLINAS RIDGE.

10 Miles From San Rafael.

C. F. LARSEN, Proprietor.

The house is located on top of Tamalpais range, 1575 feet above sea level, and commands a beautiful view of the ocean. The House has recently been considerably enlarged and refurnished. The table is first-class, and the accommodations are unsurpassed. Everything is new. Board from $1.50 to $2.00 a day; $8.00 to 10.00 per week. Send for circular. The Bolinas stage passes the place.

Postoffice address,   C. F. LARSEN,
                                  Box 958, San Rafael.

On Saturday the fire had crossed the Bolinas and San Rafael road, and the heat and flame were so intense that the stage driver was obliged to tie his wheels and leave the road, taking his chances in sliding down the naked ridge. This he accomplished in safety. But he is now carrying the mail in a cart, and does not try to run the stage. Eight bridges are reported to have been destroyed.

The fire burned to within a few feet of Summit House, but the employees and guests managed to save the inn.

The experience of cross-country skiing down a mountain in a loaded stagecoach may have proved too much for Leonard Nott, for a few weeks later he sold the stage line to Albert Sayers.

The 1900 census lists Nott as a gamekeeper in Point Reyes. In 1910 he was a roadmaster in Bolinas; in 1920 an auto driver; and in 1930 he was managing a pool hall. He died in 1933, aged 74.

The Sayers Stagecoach, 1890-1904

Albert A. Sayers was born in Bolinas in June 1861, the fifth of eight children. He worked on his father's dairy farm as a teenager, but by the age of 21 he was driving teams for Bob Cottingham's Sausalito-Bolinas stage. In 1888, aged 27, he married Mary Ellen "Mamie" Farrell, 23, of Freestone in Sonoma County. Around this time he bought the Sausalito-Bolinas Stage Line from Bob Cottingham. Two years later in 1890, like Cottingham before him, Sayers also acquired the San Rafael-Bolinas Stage Line:

> ### The Mail Stage Line Bought by Albert Sayers.
> ### A POPULAR AND PROSPEROUS ROUTE.
> The Bolinas and San Rafael mail stage line has been purchased from the owner, Leonard Nott, by Albert Sayers, of the Sausalito and Bolinas passenger and freight stage line, who will conduct both stage lines in the future. The change is an important one. Sayers is a rustler[33] from away back, and his success in conducting both stage lines cannot be doubted. The equipment and stock of the San Rafael line are excellent, but we understand Mr. Sayers will add a new, comfortable and commodious six-horse stage service next spring. Wallace Sayers, a brother of the proprietor and interested in the service, will probably handle the ribbons over the summit. For a young man he has acquired quite a reputation as a stage driver, being skillful and careful. We wish the combination success.
>
> *Marin County Tocsin*, 4 October 1890

Albert gave the job of primary driver to his younger brother, Wallace Sayers, 32. Wallace must have been good-looking, for the *Sausalito News* reported:

---

[33] An active, energetic person; not a cattle thief.

Albert Sayers, the popular proprietor of the Sausalito and Bolinas Stage line, has taken off the passenger stage on his line and is only running the freight stage. However he reports business very good. His brother Wallace, the crack driver with the smiling face, is master of transportation.

Sausalito News, 6 September 1889

The Girls Partial to Driving Over Our Fine Roads
We heard that the dashing young Bolinas stage driver, Wallace Sayers, is a great favorite in Sausalito.

Sausalito News, 8 November 1889

One of the first changes Albert Sayers made was to change the route. The Shaver Grade was washing out nearly every winter, and the long climb over the Makin Grade between Ross and San Rafael also required frequent maintenance and made for slow driving. On November 28, 1890, Sayers announced he had abandoned this route. The stage would instead make use of the Fairfax Grade. From there, it would follow the San Rafael-Olema Road (Sir Francis Drake Blvd.) to San Rafael, avoiding both steep grades—though in truth the Fairfax Grade was nearly as bad.

Without the daily stage, the San Rafael end of the Bolinas-San Rafael Road saw much less traffic and gradually fell into disuse. As of 1891, what remained was referred to as the Bolinas-Fairfax Road.

The stage line had its minor problems:

A span of Bolinas stage leaders[34] ran away on their own hook Friday. One of them struck the wheel of Engineer Dodge's buggy, at the Court House, mashing it up more or less, and driving Pete, the old black horse, against the iron hitching post, to the injury of his shoulder.

Marin Journal, 26 February 1891

George Dodge was an important man to run into. He was the County Surveyor and Engineer, replacing Hiram Austin when he was elected to the Board of Supervisors. We can only wish Pete the horse well. Still, Sayers knew how to keep his customers satisfied:

---

[34] The span leaders are the pair of horses in the front of a team.

Al Sayer's new stage takes the cake and Bolinas passengers are in high dudgeon[35] at the comfort they experience in the rapid transit. Al has a change of horses half way. A bugler is engaged for the summer.

Sausalito News, 10 April 1891

It is unclear if the bugler played a coach horn to warn away deer and other drivers, or if he served as musical entertainment on the long drive, a sort of 19th century 8-track.

Sayers also hired Thaddeus "Thad" Lewis as a driver. In June 1892, while Lewis was coming down the Fairfax Grade, the first serious accident on the road occurred:

A STAGE UPSET.
A Shying Horse Sends Bolinas Stage Off a Grade.
A NARROW ESCAPE FROM DEATH.

Ten Persons Have a Narrow Escape on the Dangerous Fairfax Grade.

On Tuesday, as the Bolinas stage was coming to San Rafael, a shying horse pulled it off the Fairfax grade, and stage, horses and passengers plunged one hundred feet down the almost perpendicular bank without injury either to passengers or horses. There were nine persons in the stage besides the driver, one man, five women and three children.

The stage, drawn by two horses, was coming down the Fairfax grade and had arrived at a place where the hill is very steep on the right hand side of the road, there being a very steep bank falling down almost perpendicularly for hundreds of feet.[36] This hill, fortunately for the passengers, is thickly wooded clear to the road-side, and about fifteen feet down the hill a strong wire fence is strung.

As the stage arrived at this place it met a painter's wagon, which had trailing behind it a long ladder, which could not be seen from the stage. As there was room to pass where the stage was, the driver hauled up, and the painter's wagon came on. Just as it was almost by, the off horse[37], a roan, saw the ladder bouncing in the dust, and with a snort, jumped to the right off the grade, and landed about four feet below on the steep hill-side. The other horse, a bay, pulled nobly to bring him up, and the roan himself seemed to realize his danger and struggled frantically to

---

[35] The editor does not seem to know that "high dudgeon" means indignation.
[36] Another report says the accident happened "100 yards below the summit of the Fairfax Grade." This would be just north of the Sky Oaks Ranger Station.
[37] The horse on the right.

regain the grade. But it was of no use. Inch by inch the bay was dragged to the edge of the grade.

The driver saw what was coming, and shouted to his passengers to jump for their lives. Three of them did so—the ladies on the front seat, and the gentleman who sat behind. Before the others could get out the bay had been pulled from the road, and then horses, stage and passengers started on a fearful plunge down the precipice.

Down through the bushes they crashed. For a moment the wire fence held the horses by their harness, but the stage turned a complete somersault over them, struck a clump of small trees, went through them, and then landed on its right side in another clump of trees where, luckily, it stayed with the horses still attached to it, flat on their sides, and quivering with pain and terror. The male passenger rushed down after the wreck and got there in time to see Lewis, the driver, with blood streaming down his face, twisting himself out of the ruins. The ladies and four of the children were then pulled out, when Lewis saw one of the children, a girl, under one of the horses, with a valise between it and the child. With a mighty tug he fairly lifted the horse up so that the male passenger could pull the child out, and when she was pulled out she stood on her feet unharmed and without a scratch on her. Wonderful to relate, not one of the passengers had any injury, in spite of the fact that they had remained in the stage which had a fearful plunge of 100 feet down an almost perpendicular precipice.

The painter, seeing the ruin he had caused, unloaded his wagon and drove here, where Mr. Robinson of the San Rafael stables sent out a 'bus to bring in the passengers. A *Journal* reporter, accompanied by Mr. McGovern, soon after arrived at the wreck, and helped Thad Lewis pull one of the horses on to his feet, and got both of them on to the grade. Beyond a few slight scratches they were uninjured. The stage is also uninjured except the top which is completely demolished.

The driver, Thad Lewis, is an old hand at the ribbons, having driven a stage for years. The writer was personally acquainted with him several years ago when he drove a stage on the difficult Forest Hill road from Auburn, and where he had a well-deserved reputation as a skillful and careful driver. No blame can be attached to him or to the stage proprietor, Mr. Al Sayers, who has never before had an accident of any kind connected with his line. In fact, this is the first accident of the kind that has ever occurred on the road since it was built, fifteen years ago.

Marin Journal, 23 June 1892

Note that the writer reported the colors of the horses, a roan and a bay, rather as we might give the makes of the cars involved in an accident. The 'bus referred to is an omnibus, a large wagon for carrying a number of people. The San Rafael Stables were at Fourth and B Streets, run by C. F. Robinson.

Liberty Ranch

In February 1892, Liberty Ranch nearly went up in flames again. As Mrs. Liberty told the reporter:

"Two peddlers called here last Friday noon and soon after they had gone I noticed a suspicious column of smoke rising skyward from the old sawmill bridge, a mile and a half from the house, at the foot of the Bolinas grade. My son Leland immediately went there to see what was the trouble, and discovered that the fire had caught the bridge at Lagunitas Creek, turned south, ascended the hill and traveled thence along the Sweet [Swede] George Creek toward Lagunitas Lake. I sent a messenger post-haste to the president of the San Rafael Water company for assistance. It was not long in coming. Fifteen men were soon on the spot, and I tell you they've been busy ever since. With their axes they cut trails through the timber, cleared a circle round the fire, and with their coarse brush brooms swept it clean. In this way they successfully fought the fire. All night Friday and all night Saturday they worked, and, at noon to-day (Sunday) the fire was well under control."

Sausalito News, 12 February 1892

In January 1893, Albert Sayers was appointed deputy sheriff for Bolinas. He must have been a busy man. He also started building a new home near Bolinas Point.

In March the *Journal* sent a reporter to describe the road:

BOLINAS.
A Pleasant Trip to the New Boom Town.

A Magnificent Drive—Beautiful Scenery— Views From the Beach—
Incidents of the Trip.

Many of the readers of the *Journal* are familiar with the drive across the "ridge" to Bolinas. To those who are not, a few words concerning a day's drive by the writer to this quiet retreat may not come amiss.

At Fairfax the Bolinas road swings westward off the main thoroughfare, which extends on northerly, and aims for the lowest part of the ridge which rises between us and the coast. Soon the grade commences, and the road twists onward and upward on the side of the hill, affording glimpses of little valleys and glades, green with the richest of verdure, with here and there bunches of dairy cattle or horses eagerly cropping the young grass which is now strong enough to afford rich nourishment.

Four or five miles of climbing brings us to a high table land, comparatively free from brush, and affording excellent pasture. Here is the well-known Liberty ranch, a place noted for the excellence of its table and healthful surrounding. It is near here that the Academy boys from the Mount Tamalpais Military Academy camp for a week or two during the summer, and get their first taste of tent life and sentry duty. Mrs. Liberty is a capital hostess and many persons have made rapid gains in health by a few weeks' stop under her hospitable roof. Beyond Liberty's camp there comes another climb of four or five miles up the ridge proper. The ridge is very steep, but the grade of the road is comparatively light, and advantage has been taken of every spur and angle. All the way up the road winds in and out through a forest of redwoods whose shade is most grateful on a hot summer day. Springs are frequent, and here and there in a turn of the road are troughs always filled with the clearest and coldest of water, refreshing alike to man and horse.

At the summit of the ridge, and surrounded by a dense and cool redwood forest is the Summit House, kept by C. F. Larsen. It is a commodious and picturesque structure, and its wide verandas and neat and attractive appearance indicate that the reputation of this resort for comfort is well provided. Mr. Larsen is a most hospitable host, and his many guests during the summer months all speak highly of his success as a provider for the wants of the inner man.

Just below the summit we get our first glimpse of the sea. The altitude is over 1,000 feet, and the descent is so abrupt that the Pacific seems to lie at our very feet. The Farallon islands, which can be seen on a clear day from the Cliff House, near San Francisco, are plainly visible, and to one unaccustomed to distances seem to be distant not five miles. An immense ocean steamer, with all sails set, a black cloud of smoke streaming from its funnel, is heading for the Golden Gate, and every now and then the waves, which are following her fast, break against the stern and roll off on the side in a mass of white foam. Several deep-water ships are visible, some coming and others going to sea—some heading northwest, some southwest. Some may be going to China, some around the Horn to Liverpool or New York; some may be going forth never to return.

Marin Journal, 2 March 1893

Larsen's Summit House. The driver may be Larsen. Courtesy of the Jack Mason Museum of West Marin History.

In July 1893, the National Guard unit Company D, First Regiment, hiked from San Rafael to Bolinas for an eight-day exercise. It was a hot day when they climbed the ridge and arrived at Larsen's. As one of the soldiers reported:

> It is said that Larsen, at the Summit House, don't keep beer. We don't believe he does; at least when we left there we will swear he did not have a drop of anything to drink in the house, beer, whiskey, or anything else. Whew! but we were dry.
>
> *Marin Journal*, 20 July 1893

Larsen might well have regretted that this soldier's story made the paper. The week before he had been arrested for selling liquor without a license. Since he was licensed four years earlier, it must have expired.

A torrential rainstorm in January 1894 caused several massive landslides in Bolinas. The Sayers' new house, still under construction, was destroyed, along with all their furniture. Undeterred, in May Sayers opened "a first-class coffee saloon, ice cream, etc. on the side."

> *Sausalito News*, 11 May 1894

In August 1894, a tragic incident occurred at Liberty's. Two teenage boys from San Rafael, William Curlett and Ralph Prescott, were hunting deer high on the mountain when Prescott's Winchester accidentally went off, shooting Curlett in the groin, severing an artery. Terrified, Prescott rushed to Liberty's for help. Vincent Liberty telephoned the doctor in San Rafael:

> The doctor had a ride of twelve miles to cover before he could reach the scene of the accident. Arriving there, Curlett was found dead, having bled to death. Young Prescott was devotedly attached to his friend and was wild with grief. He was also afraid of legal prosecution, though the Sheriff reassured him on that point. While the families of both boys recognize the purely accidental character of the shooting, they are nevertheless plunged into the deepest grief.
>
> *Sausalito News*, 24 August 1894

In August, Larsen decided to give up the Summit House and offered it for sale. Apparently there were no offers, because in November he leased a hotel in San Rafael:

Mr. C. F. Larsen has leased the Cosmopolitan Hotel, Second and B, and will open it Dec. 1st under the name of Larsen's Villa. He has thoroughly renovated the house and will keep it up to his high standard. Mr. Larsen has made an enviable name as a purveyor at the Summit House. He will continue to run the latter house, or would prefer to rent it.

Marin Journal, 22 November 1894

The Ackley Stagecoach

In April 1895 brothers Henry C. and Charles F. Ackley started an opposition stage line to Bolinas. They took on Tom McGovern as partner and driver and undercut Sayers' rates, offering a round trip for two dollars. But almost immediately they had problems:

T. A. McGovern had a narrow escape from what might have been a terrible accident. Mr. McGovern, as is well known, drives the opposition stage line between Bolinas and San Rafael. When in Bolinas recently Mr. McGovern left his team, in a hurried way, to deliver the mail. He was hardly inside Gibson's store before the four horses started on a dead run. Fortunately, two courageous young men, whose modesty prevents a mention of their names, stopped the animals in their wild course before any serious results occurred.

Sausalito News, 11 May 1895

The accident occurred outside the store of Henry Gibson, founder of the Bolinas-San Rafael Stage. Only a month later, the new stage had another accident:

Thrown From a Stage.

SAN RAFAEL, Cal., June 17.— As the Bolinas stage was coming to this city today the horses became frightened at a train at the foot of the Fairfax grade and upset the stage. The driver, Thomas McGovern, who is also owner of the stage, and a young boy by the name of Buker were thrown out, both receiving a number of cuts and bruises.

San Francisco Call, 18 June 1895

Two months after it started, the new stage line terminated service and the partnership was dissolved. Al Sayers had the road to himself again. In July 1895, Sayers discontinued the Sausalito-Bolinas stagecoach after a quarter century of service. He increased the San Rafael-Bolinas schedule to daily service each way.

On July 18, 1896, the *Marin County Tocsin* published an alarming article about an accident on the stagecoach line:

Bolinas Stage Upset.

Just before going to press news reaches us of a serious accident on the Bolinas Ridge, near Liberty's, at 10 a. m., Friday morning, the result of a collision between the Bolinas stage and a private conveyance, with several occupants. Mr. Sears [sic], the stage driver, states that he was driving down the grade with four horses, when suddenly turning a bend in the road he collided with a horse and buggy, containing two ladies and a gentleman. The stage horses got tangled up with the buggy and horse, which resulted in throwing it over the embankment. One of the ladies of the party were severely hurt, and she was taken to the Liberty ranch where medical assistance was summoned. The vehicle was completely demolished and the horse was hurt beyond recovery. The names of the parties could not be ascertained, other than one was an invalid.

In spite of all the specifics of the accident and its attribution to Sayers, in the following issue on July 25, the *Tocsin* retracted the entire story:

Bolinas Stage Not Upset.

An item appeared in the last issue of the *Tocsin* to the effect that the Bolinas Stage had suffered an accident in the way of an upset. It appears to have been an occurrence that did not occur. From an investigation of the facts, it appears that nothing of the kind happened and the wrath of the proprietor of the stage line has been stirred up to correspond. We greatly regret the error that was made. All that can be said in apology is that the story came to the office through a responsible source and was published in good faith. Mistakes of this sort will occur from time to time and we are powerless to do more than make a proper retraction and express our regret.

We can only wonder at the source of this "occurrence that did not occur." No wonder Sayers was angry about the report. But he had other problems as well.

The Scenic Railway

There had long been talk of building a railroad to the top of Mount Tamalpais. The main proponent was Louis L. Janes, Director of the Tamalpais Land and Water Company. He found backing from Sydney Cushing, President of the San Rafael Gas and Electric Company, and Albert Emmett Kent (1830-1901), a major landowner in the area. Finally, in February 1896, construction started at the train station in Mill Valley and in only six months the crews of laborers built the famously corkscrew route up the south side of the mountain to East Peak. Although the summit lay only two miles from Mill Valley as the vulture flies, the road was over eight miles long and contained 266 turns— enough to make 42 complete circles. It was billed as The Crookedest Railroad in the World. The railroad company built the Tamalpais Tavern just below the summit, offering drinks and dining on its wide verandahs overlooking San Francisco Bay, as well as comfortable lodging.

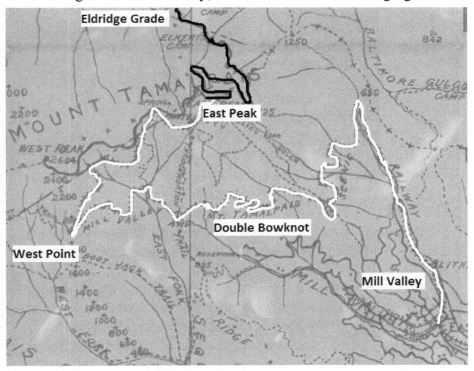

Scenic Railway and Eldridge Grade on the 1902 Tourists' Map.

The Mill Valley and Mount Tamalpais Scenic Railway was an immediate success. Tourists came from all over the world. They arrived in Sausalito by ferry from San Francisco, stepped onto the train to Mill Valley, where they walked across the platform to the Scenic Railway, and in less than an hour could be at the Tamalpais Tavern, enjoying drinks and fine food on the wide verandahs and enjoying the spectacular views. Since the entire line was one long grade, for the trip down, the open gravity cars were allowed to roll down through the redwoods with only a brakeman at the controls, a unique and thrilling experience. Millions of people came to ride the famous railroad.

The railroad and the hotel provided much easier and faster access to the scenic mountain than by taking the stage to Liberty's or Summit House and hiking the long ridge to the summit. This must have reduced business for both the stagecoach and the resorts. Worse, there were plans to build an extension from the Scenic Railway to Bolinas, eliminating the need for the stagecoach entirely.

Sayers' troubles continued. In August 1898, Secretary Case of the Society for the Prevention of Cruelty to Animals rode in the stage and noticed that one of the horses had a sore shoulder. He had Sayers fined five dollars. And in September:

ATTACKED BY AN ENRAGED BUCK
A Thrilling Combat on Bolinas Ridge.
MAN AND HORSE IN PERIL
GORED BY A MONARCH OF THE GLEN.
Peculiar Circumstances of the Encounter and Lucky Stroke That Turned the Tide of Battle.

SAN RAFAEL. Sept. 20.— Albert Sayers, proprietor of the San Rafael and Bolinas stage line, had an encounter with an enraged deer last evening that almost resulted in the loss of his life. The circumstances of the case are most peculiar.

About 5 o'clock in the afternoon Sayers was passing down a wooded slope on Bolinas ridge in a buggy when an enraged buck bounded out of the brush and ran into a wheel of the vehicle with such force that it was thrown to the ground. Maddened with the pain of the collision, it rose to its feet and ran at the horse, trying to thrust its horns into the animal's side. Fearing that his horse, a valuable animal, would be disemboweled, Sayers drew a pocket-knife and leaped out of the buggy. At the first jab

110

of the knife the infuriated buck turned on Sayers, who was knocked down by the fierce onslaught. He managed to secure a hold on one of the antlers and tried to cut the deer's throat, but could not get in an effectual blow. The struggle was so furious that Sayers was soon winded and nearly at the mercy of the angry buck, when a lucky opportunity presented itself and he drove the knife deep into its neck. At this juncture the deer gave the whistle peculiar to its species, and, with a parting stroke of its hoof that gashed Sayers' hand, broke away and fled into the forest. During the encounter the horse stood perfectly still, evidently palsied with fright. Its sides were badly torn by the buck's horns, and Sayers himself suffered numerous cuts and bruises and had his trousers shredded by the deer's hoofs.

San Francisco Call, 21 September 1898

Just another day at the office for the indomitable Sayers. That very same week, his stagecoach was robbed (see the next chapter).

Summit House

In October 1897, C. F. Larsen moved from the Summit House to Bolinas. He leased the inn to Major Henry A. Cobb, who began his tenure with an excellent decision. He hired as his chef and partner Constantine De Sella (sometimes Decilla), a Greek immigrant who had fled the troubles of Greece's War of Independence. Arriving in Marin in the early 1850s, he soon made a name for himself preparing food for the commuters on the steam ferries *Princess* and *San Rafael* between Sausalito and the City. Consi, as he was known throughout the county, had a thick flowing white beard, was well educated, and could quote long passages from Byron by

Constantine De Sella at the Summit House. Courtesy of Mill Valley History Room

memory. He brought his reputation and culinary skills to the rustic little inn, and he made it famous for its dining room.

Mr. Cobb ran the place less than a year. On October 6, 1898, the *Journal* reported:

Mr. Cobb has left the Summit House to take a business position in San Francisco, but has left the resort in the care of his partner, Prince Constantine, who makes it one of the most inviting and agreeable stopping places to be found in the county. Constantine is a prime caterer. For forty years he has tickled the palates of our bon vivants besides being personally hale fellow well met, by all, and no one can pass the Summit without calling on him. It is quite a fad to drive up there for dinner, Constantine, having telephone notice, and parties going for dinner sometimes stay for days. Large additions to the house will soon be required to accommodate the increasing patronage.

De Sella ran the Summit House for five years. In early 1903 he sold it and established a new inn called the Bolinas Ridge Tavern at Steep Ravine (probably near Pantoll). The purchaser of the Summit House was a young

Englishman named George Arthur Cranfield (1869-1949). He was a celebrated athlete and a veterinarian specializing in horses, dogs, and game fowls. He kept a kennel and bred greyhounds and fox terriers. He once entered 127 greyhounds in a San Francisco Kennel Club show. In June of 1903, he married Leah Edith Davies (1874-1946), from Galt in Sacramento County. After a brief honeymoon, they moved into the Summit House. They refurnished the place and opened for business. If their ad is to be believed, they also raised the place three hundred feet (it's at 1500 feet).

Liberty Ranch

Vincent and Mary Jane Liberty separated in 1891 and he and their daughter Elodia moved to Contra Costa County, leaving Mary Jane to run the ranch. In 1892, she hired a teenaged Swiss-Italian gamekeeper to manage the hunting side of the resort. Severino Pezzaglia, usually referred to as Sam, was born in Switzerland in 1872. He proved to be capable and hardworking and gradually assumed more responsibility until he was managing the entire operation. In 1898 Sam married Marcia Clarke, yet another granddaughter of Gregorio Briones and niece of Leonard Nott, the former owner and driver of the stage coach. Within months of their marriage, the newlyweds took on the task of running the resort alone:

> The Liberty resort on the Lagunitas, one of the best known country boarding houses in Marin County, has been reopened under the management of S. Pezzaglia. The establishment has been nearly refurnished throughout and will be found a charming residence during the spring and summer months.
>
> *Marin County Tocsin*, 19 March 1898

LIBERTY SUMMER RESORT

Newly furnished and renovated throughout........New management. Cuisine the best. Excellent accommodations for summer boarders at reasonable terms. Grandest of mountain scenery, picturesque drives and the finest climate in California. 25 minutes drive from railroad station. Telephone in house. Address for particulars......
S. PEZZAGLIA, Prop., Ross Station,

Their timing was unfortunate. Two weeks later, on March 30, 1898, a violent magnitude 6.5 earthquake centered at Mare Island rocked Marin, knocking over chimneys, cracking foundations, and dumping store shelves on the floors. Fissures appeared in the ground in Nicasio and Novato, and a mountain spring gushed out of the road between Bolinas and Summit, closing the road until it could be repaired. Whether Liberty's and Summit House were damaged is not recorded, but with the stagecoach stopped, business must have suffered.

The new century turned, but Al Sayers' luck did not. In January 1901, his wife Mamie sued for divorce. And he must have had money problems as well. In October he took out mortgages on his livery stable in Bolinas and the San Rafael-Bolinas Stage Line. In February 1902, a severe gale caused extensive damage on the Bolinas-Fairfax Road and again travel was stopped. In April there was talk of another opposition San Rafael-Bolinas stage line being established by Joseph Charles Longley (1876-1961) and Henry Strain, two young men of Bolinas, though apparently nothing came of it.

Meanwhile the construction of the new railroad line from West Point to Willow Camp continued, threatening Sayers' stage business. By April 1903 the roadbed was completed. But to the dismay of the residents of Bolinas, the plan to provide rail service to Bolinas was scrapped and the road was made for vehicles only (now Old Stagecoach Road and the Panoramic Highway).

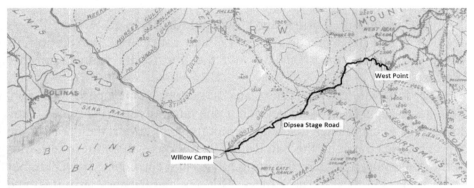

The Dipsea Stage Road from West Point to Willow Camp on the 1902 Tourist map.

The Dipsea Stage heading toward West Point in 1903. From the Ted Wurm / Fred Runner collection.

This was little comfort to Al Sayers, for in 1904 a rival stage line was established on the new Dipsea Road, a much shorter and faster alternative to his line. The new line was to be called the Dipsea Stage Line, run by County Supervisor Charles Dowd. A stable was built at West Point for the stage and horses. People from the city bound for Bolinas could now take the train to West Point and the Dipsea Stage to the coast.

With mounting marital and financial difficulties, Albert Sayers decided to sell his stagecoach business and concentrate on running his livery stable. In June 1904 he sold the line to his younger brother Wallace.

The following year, Albert and a partner went up to Tonopah, Nevada, to see if they could get rich in the huge silver strike there. They couldn't, and came back disgusted a month later. Albert then bought the Marin Stables opposite the San Rafael Courthouse, the eastern terminus of the stage line, and started renting horses and carriages. In September 1905, he leased the Flagstaff Inn in Bolinas, the western terminus, and went into hotel keeping.

Now, about that robbery I mentioned earlier.

The Stagecoach Robbery, 1898

On the morning of Monday, September 19, 1898, driver Wallace Sayers arose as usual at his home in Bolinas. He had an early breakfast, then walked across the street to the Sayers stable. The low fog still hadn't cleared and the sea air was chill. He hitched up his team, then threw open the doors of the stable, climbed up on the high seat, and drove the stage out onto Wharf Road. At exactly seven o'clock, he pulled up in front of the Flagstaff Inn, a long two-story building backing onto the lagoon. A wide porch ran along the front, and several people waited there with luggage piled at their feet.

Sayers climbed down and collected the tickets from the passengers. There was Lucas Codagan, a coachman; Mrs. Hutchinson; and salesman Ollie Stewart and his wife, all returning to San Francisco from holidays in Bolinas. There was also a young woman, Miss Annie Gordon of San Rafael, returning from visiting friends in Bolinas. The sixth passenger was Long Sing, a Chinese cook from the Flagstaff Inn, heading to the city to spend his accumulated wages. The passengers found seats, several wrapping up in blankets against the chill morning air. A hotel bellhop loaded the passengers' luggage into the boot in back.

Sayers cracked the whip and the stage moved off down the dirt main street of town, a cloud of dust rising behind. They climbed the rise out of town and down into a valley known as Gospel Flat because three churches had been built there. Reaching the base of the ridge, the two horses leaned into their work, hauling the loaded stage up the steep and twisting road.

As the day warmed and the views opened up over Bolinas Bay, the passengers started to chat and get to know one another—except Long Sing, who sat in the back and spoke to no one.

The stage crested the ridge and Sayers turned into the redwood grove and pulled up in front of Summit House. Consi De Sella came out of the kitchen to greet Wallace, but there were no passengers for the stage, so

Sayers turned the team and started down the long grade. Near the bottom they crossed the bridge over Cataract Creek, but the water was very low in late summer and the famous cataracts made barely a murmur.

The stage now came out of the dark forest into the sunny meadows along Lagunitas Creek. They passed the red gate marking the entrance to the homestead of F. C. Peters, and glimpsed below the swimming bowers he had built.

Sayers drove over the bridge, the wheels rumbling on the wide planks, and turned up the road along the right bank of the creek. He pointed out to the passengers some of the cabins barely visible under the trees along the creek. On their left, a track led up to Lily Lake, formed by an immense landslide centuries before and a favorite with anglers.

The stage arrived at Liberty's at 9 o'clock and stopped to water the horses and let the passengers buy snacks from Marcia Pezzaglia. After a brief rest, they loaded up again and continued on toward Fairfax. As the road turned north away from the creek and started the climb across the Jory Ranch toward Fairfax, it crossed a wooden bridge called Cattle Bridge over a small creek. A massive live oak beside the road cast a deep shade over the scene.

As Sayers approached this bridge, a man stood up from under the oak and stepped out to block the road. He wore a black slouch hat, striped trousers, and a long-skirted Prince Albert coat turned inside out. A red bandanna around his face allowed only his eyes to be seen. He raised a revolver and pointed it at Sayers' head.

"Put your hands up!" he shouted. Sayers reined in and hauled on the brake lever, bringing the coach to a sudden stop. He raised his hands, but one of the horses became frightened and reared, threatening to run.

Sayers called to the robber, "I can't hold him!" The man stepped forward and caught the horse's bridle. "I'll hold him," he said. "You do as I say! Keep your hands up where I can see 'em. Everybody out of the coach."

Sayers and the passengers climbed down and stood in a trembling line, their hands over their heads. The man waved the gun at Sayers. "Search the men," he ordered. "Take their wallets and watches and anything else of value and pile it up right there. Ladies, you won't be harmed," he added. There was nothing to be done. Mumbling his apologies, Sayers searched the men and took gold watches from two of them, plus a few bills and change. The robber then searched Sayers and took the stage fares from him. It only added up to about twenty dollars.

He was clearly angry at the poor takings, and he searched the men himself, finding a ten-dollar bill in one man's pocket. He stuffed the handful of loot into a pocket, then waved the gun again. "Everybody get back on the stage." When everyone was seated again, he told Sayers, "Drive on! And if anyone even turns his head to look back, I'll blow it off!"

Sayers released the brake and whistled to the team and they started off. Sayers cracked his whip and put the team into a dead run. When they had climbed a few hundred yards up the road, they turned around and looked back. The robber was walking into the woods along the creek, apparently headed toward Ross.

While the passengers described their emotions and their relief at surviving the encounter, Sayers kept the team running hard. They crested the hill and started down the Fairfax Grade. Anxious as he was to reach town, Sayers had to slow the team to a walk on this dangerous downgrade. When they reached level ground, however, he whipped up the team again. They thundered through Fairfax and skittered around the turn at the saloon, throwing up clouds of dust. They hit the San Rafael-Olema Road and high-tailed for San Rafael.

Now that the crisis was over, they fell to speculating about the robber's identity. The girl, Annie Gordon, said she thought he seemed familiar, but she couldn't be sure. Then Sayers called back over his shoulder that he had recognized the voice as that of Jesse Colwell's youngest boy Victor. Annie Gordon immediately agreed. She knew Victor well, having gone through school with him.

The stage roared through San Anselmo and entered San Rafael. Sayers maintained his speed all the way to the Marin Stable, then reined in his exhausted team. A stable boy ran out to take care of the horses, while Sayers sent another sprinting across the street to the courthouse, where the sheriff's office was in the basement. A crowd gathered around the stage to see what all the commotion was about. As the men helped the ladies down from the stage, everyone was talking at once, telling about their terrifying experience.

Minutes later Sheriff Henry Harrison arrived on the scene, accompanied by Constable Louis Hughes. They quickly learned what had happened. It was just eleven o'clock, and when he heard the robber was apparently on foot and headed for Ross, he called for a posse. A number of men in the crowd volunteered. Within minutes, the sheriff selected a Mr. Harrison, George Agnew, James Gordon (possibly

Annie's father), and Isaac Smith. They hurried off for their horses. While Constable Hughes fetched their own horses, the Sheriff got a rough list of the stolen items.

Long Sing appeared very pleased. "Me very cute!" he crowed. "I have much money hidden in inside pocket, but robber no find because I have so many pockets." Codagan reported that he had $100 in a small purse on his belt that the robber missed.

The Sheriff then asked for a description of the robber and Sayers and the passengers agreed on the details of his clothing. The coat turned inside-out was a puzzle, but the Sheriff said he assumed that was done so the coat wouldn't be identified.

As the posse began to gather and Hughes arrived with the horses, Sayers took the Sheriff aside and told him of his suspicion that the robber was Victor Colwell. The Sheriff was surprised, but just nodded.

The posse of six wheeled their horses and thundered down Fourth Street and out of town. When they reached Ross, the Sheriff asked the stationmaster if he had seen a man answering the description. He described seeing Victor Colwell go by only twenty minutes before, on foot and appearing to be in a hurry.

The Sheriff thanked him and the posse hurried on. About halfway to Greenbrae, they overtook a man walking along the road. He wore striped trousers, a black slouch hat, and a long coat. They reined in beside him. It was Victor Colwell. He looked up at the Sheriff in surprise, glancing at the grim-faced men with him.

The Sheriff said they were looking for a prisoner who had escaped from San Quentin. Colwell said he had seen no one suspicious. Then the Sheriff dismounted and stood before him. He told Colwell there had been a holdup of the Bolinas stage a little while ago, out by Liberty's.

Colwell at first tried to deny it, but the Sheriff told him he would have to come with them. Constable Hughes swung Colwell up onto the back of his horse and they rode back to Ross station, where they met Wallace Sayers riding fast.

As soon as he saw Colwell, Sayers identified him as the man who had held them up. They dismounted and went into the station, where Hughes searched Colwell's pockets. In one was a .38-calibre Smith & Wesson. In the other was a red bandanna tied into a bundle. Inside were two watches and a handful of bills and coins.

Colwell immediately confessed to the crime, saying he had been fired from his job on the railroad for drunkenness and was out of work and hungry. One ten-dollar gold piece was not one of the items stolen, and Colwell said it was his. When the Constable asked him why he robbed the stage when he had money, Colwell said, "I didn't want to get down to my last bean."

The posse transported Colwell back to San Rafael, where the other passengers identified him and their stolen articles. Colwell was put into a corner cell in the San Rafael jail, one that was reputed to be haunted by a ghost[38]. The Sheriff telephoned the Colwell family home to break the bad news. Then the 28-year-old Colwell broke down and sobbed. "O God! This is terrible on my poor mother and sister."

The robbery created a sensation because he came of such a good family. His parents Jesse and Mary Jane Colwell were respectable and well-liked. His father was a road-builder—in fact, he had built the road where the holdup occurred.

Two months passed and the trial had not yet begun. A suspect was supposed to be released if not

HOLD-UP OF THE BOLINAS STAGE.

tried within sixty days. The *San Francisco Call* blamed the delay on the inefficiency of District Attorney Ennio Martinelli: "Highwaymen Nearly Turned Loose Again."

Victor's attorney James Cochrane filed a writ of Habeas Corpus to have him released, but Martinelli filed a new charge and the writ was denied. In November, a new District Attorney, Hugh McIsaac, was elected. In January, a new sheriff was appointed, Will Taylor. A few days later, Victor asked to see Sheriff Taylor:

---

[38] That of petty thief William F. Argo, who hanged himself in the cell on January 10, 1890. His ghost was reported half a dozen times over the next ten years.

YOUNG BANDIT'S HEART PREVAILS
Abandons Attempt to Be Free.
COLWELL IN GALLERY ROLE
HAD CELL BARS ALMOST CUT IN TWO
Marin County's Youthful Highwaymen Sends for Sheriff Taylor and
Surrenders Several Smuggled Tools.

SAN RAFAEL, Jan 25. Victor J. Colwell, the youthful bandit, who held up
the stage running between this city and Bolinas last September, came
within an ace of regaining his liberty and taking French leave of this
community a few nights ago. Saws for cutting steel were smuggled in to
him by confederates, and when he ceased work he had four bars of the
window in his cell nearly sawed through. A few hours' work was all that
stood between him and freedom, but, strange to say, a debt of gratitude
he owed to Will P. Taylor, the new Sheriff, so preyed upon his mind that
at the last moment he revealed the fact of his intended jailbreak, and
handed over his tools to the officers of the law.

San Francisco Call, 26 January 1899

The trial finally began January 30, 1899, nearly five months after the
robbery. But there were long delays finding unbiased jurors, in spite of
the Colwell family's respectable reputation:

YOUTHFUL BANDIT'S WILY INSANITY DODGE
Why Difficulty Is Experienced in Obtaining Jurors to Try Victor Colwell.

SAN RAFAEL, Feb. 6.— Twenty-five men out of a venire[39] of thirty took
the stand in the Superior Court to-day and were immediately disqualified
from acting as jurors on account of having formed a positive opinion that
young Victor Colwell is guilty of the crime of highway robbery. It was
found necessary to issue orders for another venire of forty, out of which
it is hoped the remaining seven jurors can be selected, and to continue
the trial of the case to Thursday. Attorney Cochrane will try to prevent the
young bandit being sent to San Quentin by using the insanity dodge. The
feeling in Marin County runs high against him for everybody believes that
if he had met resistance in holding up the Bolinas stage he would have

---

[39] A jury panel.

122

committed murder. It is claimed that if he is insane his insanity is of long standing, for his peculations began as a boy when employed in the store of Captain H. A. Gorley.

San Francisco Call, 7 February 1899

Victor's father, mother, and sister Ida all testified that he was unstable and not responsible for his actions. But the driver Wallace Sayers and teenage passenger Annie Gordon, who knew Victor from high school, stated that he had appeared rational at the time of the robbery. The jury did not accept the insanity defense, and Victor was sentenced to seven years in San Quentin prison, where his father had been a guard. Ida as county clerk had to register her own brother as a felon.

A Seven Years Sentence.

On Monday Victor J. Colwell was sentenced to serve a term of seven years in San Quentin. His attorney moved for a new trial but Judge Angellotti denied the motion and refused to sign a writ of probable cause. Sheriff Taylor took the convict to the prison Tuesday.

Marin Journal, 23 February 1899

Victor Jesse Colwell's San Quentin mug shots

We can only imagine the shame and embarrassment Victor's long ordeal was to his parents. Throughout the long wait and the trial, his father Jesse was busy building the new road from San Rafael to Tiburon. On July 22, 1899, four months after Victor's conviction, the road was finally completed. Though the contractor lost a great deal of money on the job, it was hailed as a beautiful and well-built road. But on the very same day:

Sudden Death of Jesse Colwell.

Jesse Colwell, a pioneer resident of this county, died suddenly at his home in San Rafael on Sunday morning. Death came suddenly, and he passed away before his family realized that the fatal stroke had been struck. Mrs. Colwell was with him at the time. For a number of years he has been a road contractor, and at one time was an official at San Quentin prison. He leaves a widow, Mary A. Colwell, two sons, Grant and Victor, and one daughter, Miss Ida M. Colwell. He was highly esteemed and respected in the community.

Sausalito News, 22 July 1899

None of the reports mention the cause of death. Was Jesse's sudden death the result of Victor's conviction? Could it even have been suicide? The death must have been a crushing blow to the family, Victor included; he could not even attend his father's funeral.

The new century turned with Victor still in San Quentin. He must have been a model prisoner because he was paroled on November 16, 1903, having served three years and nine months. He got a job as a teamster at the E. K. Wood Lumber Company on San Anselmo Avenue, now the site of the San Anselmo Post Office.

He seems to have made a success of himself. Later that year he was elected a representative to the Building Trades Council. Curiously enough, he was also the music director of the "catchy spectacle" *The Black Crook*, America's first musical play, written in 1866.

As an aside, Victor's sister Ida met her husband in an unusual way. On January 23, 1908, the *Marin Journal* printed a snippy reprimand against a rival paper:

A local paper has announced that the engagement of Miss Ida Colwell and Mr. Blackledge was recently announced. The *Journal* is authorized to positively deny the report. Such unwarranted and unauthorized reports are very embarrassing to the interested parties and should not be made.

Ida, amused by the mistake, cut out the newspaper clipping and sent it to her brother Grant, then in Sonoma County. She addressed it to "G. Colwell, Forestville, California." The letter was mistakenly delivered to George Colwell, no relation, who must have read it in some confusion. But he liked the wit and tone of the writer. He became curious and wrote back to Ida, telling her that her letter had gone astray. The two corresponded, met, fell in love, and married. She didn't even have to change her name.

Victor's brother Grant, the Spanish-American war hero, died at age 51 in Los Angeles. Ida and George moved to Suisun and her mother Mary Jane and her brother Victor joined them there. By the 1930 census the family had moved to E Street in Antioch. At that time Victor was a watchman in a paper mill. He died in Antioch in 1934, aged 63. Four years later, Mary Jane died, aged 95. In 1941, Ida died at 63. Her husband George lived to be 88, dying in Napa in 1965.

So all the Colwells were gone and they left no descendants. Their only lasting memorial is the beautiful Bolinas-Fairfax Road.

But it was soon to undergo some substantial changes.

Tamalpais and Phoenix Dams, 1903-1906

Tamalpais Dam

Water had always been a crucial concern in Marin County. The Spanish chose the site of their San Rafael Mission for the same reason the Miwok had built their village Awani-wi there—the reliable year-round Old Mission Spring just above it. As the county developed following the gold rush, several entrepreneurs built small dams on the creeks on their land and sold the water to their neighbors. Eventually many of these small operations merged into the Marin County Water Company, owned by a number of wealthy and influential landowners. Its president and founder was William Tell Coleman, who owned large tracts in San Rafael and developed the Coleman Addition (today's Dominican neighborhood). He was also a leader of the anti-Chinese movement and president of the San Francisco Committee of Vigilance, which lynched eight accused criminals.

In 1873 the Water Company constructed Lagunitas Dam and piped the water to San Rafael. They built a small dam in Bill Williams Gulch in 1886 and another in Swede George Canyon in 1888, but these dams only tapped small creeks and provided limited amounts of water. Lake Lagunitas was the only large reservoir and its level varied considerably with the seasonal rains. The first years of the twentieth century were some of the driest on record and the lake fell to alarming levels. On October 23, 1903, the water company sent out a harsh notice to its customers:

"Inasmuch as our water consumers are not cooperating as requested, in assisting the company to husband the short supply of water in Company's reservoirs, and do not seem to recognize the gravity of the situation, we beg to notify each and every consumer, that unless strict regard is given

126

to Company's requests, the present supply of water in the Lake will last but a short period and the whole community will be without water."

It was not a matter of not enough rainfall—then as now, heavy winter rains produced more water than could be used. The problem was inadequate storage capacity. Lagunitas Lake held only 341 acre-feet. In a storm, it would quickly fill and the excess water would pour down the wooden flume and down Lagunitas Creek to the Pacific, lost for human use.

In 1903, the water company started planning a new dam a mile downstream from Lake Lagunitas on the old Bontempi Dairy property they had bought in 1878. They would have preferred a site farther downstream, but that area was owned by the Shafter-Howard family, who hoped to develop a reservoir there themselves and refused to sell. The company proposed building the new Tamalpais Dam as far downstream as they could, right on the border with the Shafter-Howard land. It was not an ideal site—the valley there was broad and flat and there was little bedrock to anchor the new dam. To impound enough water, the dam would have to be a massive structure eight hundred feet long and seventy feet high, requiring 300,000 cubic yards of soil. Also, because of the flat topography, the new reservoir would spread out wide.

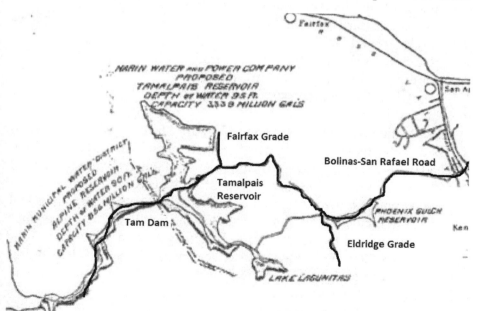

1916 Marin Water and Power Company map of proposed reservoirs. Courtesy MMWD.

The southern arm, roughly where Bon Tempe Reservoir is today, would reach the foot of Lagunitas Dam. The northern portion would flood the flat terrace where the Meadow Club golf course is today. This area dropped away to the east, so the project also called for two smaller dams to keep the reservoir from overflowing down Shaver and Fish gulches. It would be a large expensive multi-year project, but the resulting lake would add more than ten thousand acre-feet, increasing the existing storage by thirty times.

Construction began in the summer of 1903 with the digging of trenches on either side of the valley for the massive concrete abutments to support the new dam.

The new lake would also require re-routing a half-mile of the Bolinas-San Rafael road. Road viewers were hired and they determined that simply running the road along the edge of the new lake would create erosion and sedimentation problems and perhaps pollute the water supply. They said the only practical route was to leave the old road just east of Liberty Ranch, zig-zag up the steep rocky north side of Liberty Gulch, then circle around Azalea Hill through the Jory Ranch to connect to the Fairfax Grade. At the urging of the water company, in March 1906 the Board of Supervisors condemned the old road from Liberty's to Jory's.

Excavation for the north abutment of Tamalpais Dam. Photo by author.

But William E. (1857-1933) and Lucy Jory (1860-1947) objected to the road across their land. They had recently opened their Redwood Inn and had plans to expand their operation. They claimed the proposed road would destroy three springs and a proposed private reservoir site, as well as some valuable redwood and other timber. The water company asked the county to condemn the right-of-way for the public good. The county agreed, and offered the Jorys $1,500 in damages for a 3000-foot right-of-way across their land. They refused and sued the county, demanding $50,000 in damages—well over a million dollars in today's money. The case dragged on for over a year.

Meanwhile, the Shafter-Howard family—more like a business consortium, including Stanford University—got into the game. They owned the land just downstream of the proposed Tamalpais Dam (and all the way out to the tip of Point Reyes). They formed their own company, the Lagunitas Water Company, with plans to compete against the Marin County Water Company. They started planning for a dam at the site of Shaver's sawmill and another several miles farther downstream to be called San Geronimo Dam. They filed a lawsuit against the water company, saying it was taking water that should be allowed to flow into their land. They published engineers' reports claiming that their rival's Tamalpais Dam was a poor site with porous soils and inadequate watershed. A bitter debate flared in the newspapers, with each company accusing the other of lying and underhanded dealings. The future of the project became even more uncertain. In October 1903, construction was halted on the Tamalpais Dam. The affected section of the Bolinas-Fairfax had been abandoned by the County, but the bypass had not yet been started.

Phoenix Dam

In the meantime, the water level in Lagunitas Lake continued to drop and public pressure for more storage increased. In 1905, the Water Company proposed a smaller dam in Phoenix Gulch above Ross, to impound around 300 acre-feet. The reservoir would inundate a section of the Bolinas-San Rafael road. Surveyors determined that a replacement road above the water level of the new lake was impossible due to sedimentation and pollution concerns. It was felt that since the stagecoach route had moved to the Fairfax Grade, the road through Ross was now little used and no longer needed. In 1907 the County officially abandoned the road. The neighboring ranch owned by the estate of Janet Porteous sued, saying the abandonment cut off their access to Ross and San Rafael, forcing them to go up Shaver Grade and down the Fairfax Grade to Fairfax, a much longer and more difficult route. Finally, in April 1908 the water company bought the Porteous ranch, eliminating the need to replace the road. The Phoenix Dam was built and quickly filled, drowning the old stagecoach road. Thirty years after it was built, the Bolinas-San Rafael road had ceased to exist; only the Bolinas-Fairfax remained.

The Sayers-McCurdy Stagecoach, 1904-1905

The Bolinas-Fairfax Road in Lagunitas Valley before Alpine dam, looking north-east from above Alpine toward Liberty's. Image from the Coyne Family Collection.

Wallace Augustus Sayers was born in Bolinas in 1868 and from at least the age of 21 he worked as a driver on his older brother Albert's two stage lines. He it was who was so popular with the ladies. In 1895, aged 27, he married Susan Mary Smith (1860-1937), eight years his senior and a divorcée. The next year, they had a daughter, Mabel Ruth (1896-1980).

Hugh Ingram McCurdy was born in Bolinas on January 28, 1877. His parents were Samuel Steele McCurdy (1836-1907) and Adeline "Addie" Ingram (1855-1929), long-time Bolinas-area residents and ranchers. He was the third of fourteen children, though many died young. The same month he bought the stage lines, he married Edith Eva Gregg (1877-1932) of Fruitvale in Oakland.

In June 1904, the two men went into partnership:

MARIN STAGE LINES HAS CHANGED HANDS

Both the Dipsea and the Bolinas-San Rafael stage lines have been sold to Wallace Sayers and Hugh McCurdy, well known residents of Bolinas. The Dipsea line was owned by Supervisor C. J. Dowd and ran between West Point on Tamalpais Scenic road and Willow Camp. The other line was owned by Albert Sayers. While thus making a change in the ownership, the patrons of the lines will not notice it as they are acquainted with both of the purchasers. The lines are two of the best short stage lines in the state and the country traversed by them is the most picturesque in the county.

Marin Journal, 23 June 1904

Supervisor Dowd may have been ready to sell his Dipsea line because just six weeks earlier on May 9, 1904, there had been an attempted holdup:

MASKED BANDIT HALTS DOWDS STAGE
HIGHWAYMAN MAKES HIS APPEARANCE IN A LONELY PART OF THE ROAD
Quick Action by the Driver Harry Ashe Sends the Would-be Robber and His Gun Into the Steep Ravine.

A genuine bandit made his appearance on Mount Tamalpais a week ago last Monday and at the point of a gun attempted to stop the stage at the head of Steep Ravine on the road between West Point and the Dipsea Inn. The coolness of Harry Ashe, the driver, alone frustrated his plans and incidentally sent him sprawling into the brushy canyon.

The stage was rolling down the mountain side at a fast clip when it reached a curve in the road near the head of Steep Ravine. When this was rounded the first thing that met Driver Ashe's eyes was a man whose head was masked in a gunny sack and whose arms were pointing a shotgun directly at him. When first seen the horses were almost upon him and it took Ashe but a second to realize that he could not stop in the distance if he wanted to. Bending low, he swung his whip and the horses increased their speed. The would-be robber attempted to step to one side at the same time trying to aim his gun but he was too late, the heavy collar on the near leader crashed into him and he and the gun rolled over the embankment into the brush. It was all done in the twinkling of an

131

eye and almost before Ashe realized that an attempt had been made to hold him up. The latter continued his journey and concluded to let others hunt for the bandit. The highwayman is described as being about five feet ten inches in height and rather slightly built. The way the man acted in attempting the crime precludes the idea that he is an old timer at the holdup business for he did his work like a novice.

Marin Journal, 19 May 1904

The attempted holdup was recreated a century later in 2004 (bandit not included).
Photo courtesy of Brad Rippe.

The novice highwayman was never identified.

Buying the two stage lines must have been a major investment for the two young men—Sayers was 36 and McCurdy just 27. But Sayers was not done. The Scenic Railway, seeing the popularity of the new stage line from West Point, built a small rustic hotel there in 1904. On September 3, Sayers leased the hotel and opened the West Point Inn:

Last Saturday Wallace Sayers opened his new hotel at West Point, on the Scenic Railroad. First class accommodations and courtesy are promised, and the ideal surroundings of the hotel should help to make it a most popular resort.

Marin County Tocsin, 10 September 1904

The West Point Inn in 1904 soon after it was built. The earlier stable for the Dipsea Stage to Stinson Beach is in back. The Scenic Railway encircles the building. The couple could be Susan and Wallace Sayers. From the Ted Wurm / Fred Runner collection.

As so often in this story, their timing could not have been worse. Four days later a fire, supposedly started by the sun shining through a broken bottle, erupted behind the Hasbrouck[40] cabin near the Summit House on Bolinas Ridge. Fanned by strong northerly winds, it swept rapidly down the ridge and within 25 minutes had reached Bolinas Lagoon, burning the pastures and fields of a half-dozen ranches.

Men poured out of Bolinas to fight the fire. The flames were stopped only forty feet from the buildings on the McCurdy ranch—Hugh's parents' home. On the Bourne ranch nearby, the big trees from the ridge came down close to the buildings. When they burst into flame, the volunteers at McCurdy's piled into wagons and rushed over there:

They manned the roofs armed with wet sacks and beat out the flames as fast as they caught in the shingles. Louis Peters [Petar] undoubtedly saved the barn on one occasion. The roof was blazing in one spot and the wet sacks had no effect upon the flames. With rare presence of mind

---

[40] Joseph Hasbrouck (1840-1901), sometimes spelled Has Brouk or Hasbrouch, was a publisher of law books. He and his wife Anginette Moyle Hasbrouck (1863-1940) lived in San Francisco but owned an estate in Larkspur called "Ho Ho." In the 1890's, they bought a property just north of Summit House and built a cabin there. He killed himself in 1901.

he kicked the blazing shingles loose and with his hands threw them to the ground. It was a splendid exhibition of nerves.

Marin Journal, 15 September 1904

Among those who saved this ranch were Albert Sayers, Leonard Nott, and Hugh McCurdy, three men who had owned the San Rafael and Bolinas Stage.

The next day the fire was still completely out of control and burning toward Summit House:

By noon it was realized that the fate of the old hostelry depended entirely upon the wind. At that time L. Constantine, the proprietor, packed his chattels in a wagon and moved to Liberty ranch, five miles away, leaving one man in charge of Summit House. After 9 o'clock in the evening this man staggered into Liberty's scorched, foot-sore and weary with his hours of firefighting, with the news that the old landmark had been completely destroyed by the flames. Nearly 100 men hurriedly gathered from all parts of the county, were sent out from Liberty's last evening to fight the fire under the direction of George Martin, fire marshal for the American Forestry Association. About 7 o'clock Martin telephoned the fire had gotten over the Bolinas Ridge and was now traveling rapidly in this direction. He asked that Constable Agnew get six picked men and meet him at Liberty's as soon as possible in order to start in backfiring, and if possible save the splendid forest in Lagunitas canyon, toward which this end of the fire is now traveling. On the other side of the ridge the flames appeared to have reached Cascade canyon[41]. If it once gets a start in the heavy timber of this canyon the probabilities are that it will reach the slopes of Tamalpais, and eventually destroy the West Point Hotel on the line of the scenic railway. S. B. Cushing, manager of the Mount Tamalpais scenic railway, is working at the head of Cascade canyon with a large force of men. These fires have been burning for thirty-six hours now and for nearly that length of time there has been no telephone or telegraphic communication with Bolinas. The stage from Bolinas to San Rafael found it impossible to get through the burning district, and all mail from

---

[41] An earlier name for Cataract Canyon leading up to Rock Spring. A number of old maps show this drainage as Cascade Canyon.

that point was taken around the mountain to West Point and thence to Mill Valley, via the scenic railway.

Santa Cruz Evening Sentinel, 10 September 1904

For the next several days the wind kept changing direction, driving the fire first toward Camp Taylor, then toward the Pedrini ranch (near today's Peters Dam), then toward Mount Tamalpais, and finally toward Ross. The County Treasurer, Mr. Fallon, led a squad of men from Ross up into the hills to dig a trench across the Lagunitas Valley and stopped the flames.

Finally, after five days, the fire was brought under control. More than four thousand acres of prime timber had burned, many outbuildings were lost, and a whole season's grain and pasturage were destroyed, but no lives were lost. Only two homes were destroyed—the Hasbrouck place where the fire started, and the Summit House. It was five more days before Wallace Sayers could take the first stage through the devastated area. The big bridge over the Lagunitas, by now called Alpine Bridge, was destroyed, but a temporary road a few yards upstream allowed the stages to ford the creek.

Summit House

John Wright[42], who had purchased the Summit House property in May 1903, announced that he intended to rebuild the hotel and tavern, maintaining the log cabin style, but now with accommodations for fifty people. It re-opened in March of 1906, but it was never again successful as a roadhouse. He converted it into a private home he called Ridgecrest. Wright was a member of both the Sierra Club and the Cross Country Club. In September 1909 he erected a large flagpole on the highest point of his property and invited both clubs to attend a flag-raising ceremony. The Sierra Club hiked in from West Point and the Cross Country Club from Camp Taylor. To the singing of patriotic songs, Mrs. Wright raised the flag, said to be visible from San Francisco. The socket for the flagpole is still there. Wright died in September 1916 and the property was sold to Belle N. Petersen. The building burned down in the great fire of September 1945.

---

[42] John Malinsbury Wright (1851-1916).

135

Liberty Ranch

No doubt the Liberty Ranch felt the economic impact of the damage to their land and to the stage road from the big fire in 1904. In August 1906, Sam Pezzaglia undertook to repair the burned-out bridge at Alpine:

Sam Pezzaglia, of Liberty Ranch, has a force of men busy repairing the bridge across the Lagunitas creek. The work is being done thoroughly. Five large pine trees have been converted into big beams and these will span the creek. While these repairs are going on a temporary crossing has been made some feet east of the bridge. It's a pretty steep affair.

Marin Journal, 9 August 1906

In August 1905, Wallace Sayers sold his interest in the two stagecoach lines to his partner Hugh McCurdy. In September, Sayers and his wife joined his brother Albert in running the Flagstaff Inn in Bolinas. So the Sayers families owned the stables at both ends of the San Rafael line, the hotel at the Bolinas end, and the West Point Inn on the Dipsea line. They stood to make a lot of money from the ever-increasing flood of tourists.

Yet again, their timing was not good. Seven months later, the disastrous San Francisco earthquake struck, with two hundred miles of the San Andreas Fault breaking loose, moving Bolinas as much as thirty-two feet north:

The Earthquake in Marin County

Large fissures over a foot wide and several hundred feet long show plainly that Bolinas felt the shock very severely. Flagstaff Inn was moved several feet into Bolinas Bay. Sayers stable collapsed, preventing the stage going out. Several frame buildings will have to be rebuilt. Judge McCurdy brought the mail out on a cart and reported that the county road over Tamalpais was fissured in many places.

Sausalito News, 14 April 1906

The Flagstaff Inn was demolished and never rebuilt. Wallace Sayers' wife Susan operated a hotel in the Gibson house, and only three months after the quake, on July 12, 1906, she announced they were back in operation in time for the summer rush.

Wallace Sayers had other businesses in hand. In 1909, he made an offer to buy the wreck of the steamer *R. D. Inman*, which had run aground on Agate Beach, just north of Bolinas, but was out-bid. He and a partner, Sherman Smith, bought and subdivided the Bolinas Mesa, offering 58 lots at $500 each. The next year, the family moved to San Francisco and Sayers opened a wholesale liquor business. He built several cabins at his place in Bolinas and rented them out. Before 1920, he and Susan had divorced. He died in Bolinas on October 22, 1925, aged 57.

Bolinas Open for Business

Mrs. Wallace Sayers announces that her summer resort has been remodeled and is now in a better condition than ever to accommodate her guests. Parties desiring to visit Bolinas are requested to write to her for terms and engage rooms in advance. Fine boating, fishing and hunting. Bolinas, the ideal place to spend a summer.

Mrs. Wallace Sayers.

The McCurdy Stagecoach, 1905-1908

In August of 1905, Hugh McCurdy bought out Wallace Sayers' shares in the two stage lines. At some point he took as a partner Robert Farrell, a Bolinas saloonkeeper.

The next year, there was more trouble for the stage line:

SAN RAFAEL IS ANGERED BY CRUEL STAGE DRIVER
Pitiful Condition of Horses Driven
Over Steep Grade Causes the Constable to Act
SAN RAFAEL. Aug. 25.— Indignation is manifested here over the condition of the horses which draw the Bolinas stage which carries the United States mail.

Constable George Agnew yesterday arrested Walter Longley, driver of the stage, which is operated by a man named McCurdy. Longley is charged with cruelty to animals, and ugly abrasions on the horses' breasts offer evidence of the suffering endured by the animals. It is claimed that the two teams employed on the 22 mile pull have been driven without rest, and that in spite of their pitiful condition they had been whipped up the six mile grade which starts at Fairfax. It is probable that a severe sentence will be given both driver and owner.

San Francisco Call, 26 August 1907

There is no further mention of the incident, so perhaps charges were dropped. Let us hope Hugh McCurdy was not mistreating his horses. On New Year's Eve, there was more trouble:

Tuesday afternoon, at the corner of Fourth and B streets, the Bolinas stage ran into the buggy of Mr. B. Hoffman, who lives out on the Petaluma road, springing the axle of the buggy and bending the wheel. Mr. Hoffman

138

was driving up Fourth Street when the stage came up behind him and struck his buggy as mentioned, doing several dollars damages.

Marin Journal, 2 January 1908

Surely "several dollars damage" constituted only a minor fender-bender even in those days. Petaluma Road is now Lincoln Avenue.

A new danger threatened. Automobiles were starting to appear around the county, alarming many citizens. Horses unaccustomed to the loud smoky machines sometimes panicked, and many drivers thought them a danger. Petitions were circulated in Marin and Sonoma counties and elsewhere, proposing to ban automobiles entirely from all public roads:

PROHIBITORY ORDINANCE SIDE TRACKED
Supervisors Will Regulate Use of Automobiles.

At the session of the Board of Supervisors last Monday, all members were present except Mr. Goudy. Although the meeting was for the special purpose of considering an ordinance prohibiting the use of automobiles in this county, not one of the 400 and odd signers asking for extreme legislation put in an appearance. On the other hand, a strong and efficient delegation of automobilists from across the Bay were on deck to protest against the passage of any drastic measure. The advocates of the horseless carriage had the floor from start to finish. F. A. Hyde, president of the Automobile Club of San Francisco, was the main orator, a gentleman who has the ability to talk a bird off a bush. He made a very tactful and diplomatic plea to the Board and one that evidently made an impression. He strongly favored proper restrictions and regulation, while pointing out the impractibility and in fact impossibility of absolute prohibition in view of the decision of Superior Judge Lennon. He agreed that many roads in Marin county should not be opened to automobiling. All that was desired was liberty to use the main highways. He also favored any measure that would keep reckless drivers out of the county. Most of the prejudice against automobiles arose from the acts of a few outlaws in the business who ran their machines with a total disregard to the rights of the public. No one, he said, wanted them suppressed more earnestly than the decent men who patronized the sport. Answering a member of the Board, Mr. Hyde said that he thought a license system would work well and that he was heartily in favor of it.

But the new "automobilists" ("drivers" drove horses) especially enjoyed the scenic drive to Bolinas. Sam Pezzaglia of Liberty's was concerned enough that he wrote a letter to the *Journal* on May 7, 1908:

A JUST PROTEST

I think the automobiles should be more careful and not be allowed to travel with such speed especially on the San Rafael road where the turns are short and the roads narrow. I have met some that have come around the turns so fast, that has almost caused an accident on many different occasions.

S. PEZZAGLIA.

The automobiles had their own problems:

SUPPOSED TRAGEDY ON THE BOLINAS ROAD

An automobile party coming over the mountain from Bolinas early in the morning one day last week experienced a shock by suddenly coming in contact with what appeared to be the dead body of a man in the middle of the road on a steep down grade. A scream from one of the ladies brought the machine to a standstill just about a foot from the body, which was just discernible in the haze of early morning. A stiff hat was visible, while a blanket covered the body. The party was horrified and at once jumped out of the automobile. It all indicated a dreadful tragedy. After a few moments conversation it was decided to investigate and solemnly, almost tearfully, the party stood around the victim when one of the gentlemen pulled the blanket away and found a buggy seat, a cushion, and the hat, aforesaid. Then the party breathed more freely. In fact, there was a peal of laughter that echoed through the hills.

Marin Journal, 14 May 1908

At the same time, the Marin County Water Company announced plans to build a dam in Lagunitas Valley that would submerge the Bolinas-Fairfax road. This could mean the end of the Bolinas-San Rafael Stage. Perhaps discouraged at the business prospects, in March 1908 Hugh McCurdy sold his half-share of the stage lines to Albert Sayers, the man who had run it for fourteen years.

In May, McCurdy paid $3,500 for the Murray Stables on C Street in San Rafael. He remained in the livery business for many years, later worked for the water company, and died in San Rafael in 1932, aged fifty-five.

The Second Sayers Stagecoach, 1908-1911

True to his luck, Albert Sayers soon had problems. In April 1909, his wife filed divorce proceedings—for the second time in eight years:

Mamie Sayers, through her attorney Mr. K. Hawkins, has instituted divorce proceedings against her husband Albert Sayers a prominent citizen of Bolinas. Their marital life has been far from being congenial.

Sausalito News, 17 April 1909

On September 18, 1909, the *Marin County Tocsin* reported:

Albert Sayers Buys Interest in Stage

Albert Sayers, one of the original owners of the Bolinas stage, has purchased a half interest in the line from the present owner, Robert Farrell. The sale went into effect last Monday. Mr. Sayers is a veteran at the business and Mr. Farrell has proven himself a popular and capable proprietor of a business, the good operation of which is of vital importance to the traveling public. The stage ride to Bolinas is one of the finest trips in the state. For three hours the great coach and four follow the winding road over the ridges and through the canyons finally descending on the western slope of the main ridge to Bolinas. On the trip marine and woodland views are in constant rivalry, challenging the admiration. Each year more people are learning of the attractiveness of the trip and each year sees an increase in the travel.

So Albert Sayers had bought out both Hugh McCurdy and Robert Farrell and was again sole proprietor of the lines he had run so long.

A serious accident occurred in December 1909 when the Bolinas stage was passing Liberty's:

BOLINAS STAGE GOES
THROUGH FRAIL BRIDGE

Last Thursday morning at about nine o'clock as the Bolinas stage, loaded with four passengers and the driver, was coming to this city on its daily trip, a bridge near the Liberty ranch about ten miles from this city collapsed, owing to the recent heavy rains, and the passengers narrowly escaped with their lives. When the party was about a mile from the bridge it encountered a deputy

road inspector who informed the driver, Jack Frazier, that all was "O. K." and that the bridge was safe, so when the stage arrived at the bridge, it proceeded to cross and, when in the middle, the frail bridge collapsed, forming a V. The occupants, Mrs. Una Allbright of Bolinas, John Strain, Alexander Mendotte, A. L. Jenkins and Jack Frazier, were all thrown out. Mrs. Albright landed on the plunging horses and it was a miracle that she was not frightfully mangled, but as it was, she was not injured, only sustained a severe shock. John Strain of Bolinas, who was on his way to San Francisco, was the most unlucky one of the five. In some manner his head was caught under the brake-block and he sustained numerous cuts and bruises. The stage started to slide into the water and just as the unfortunate man was about to be dragged under the water, where he would have met death by drowning, the stage stopped its downward flight. Owing to the weight of the stage, it took some time to extract the unfortunate man from his perilous position and in doing so, it was necessary to relieve him of his coat. A. L. Jenkins, manager of the Lagunitas Rod and Gun Club, had only ridden on the stage about a mile, having gotten on at the Club House. He was thrown clear of the wreck and sustained only a few bruises. While he was thrown clear of the stage, some egg cases followed him and pinned his legs in the "V" shape of the wreck and it was some minutes before he could extract himself and run back to the Club House, where he telephoned for assistance. In a short space of time help came and two buggies, one lent by a neighbor and one from a local livery stable, took the passengers to San Rafael. Jack Strain, who was injured quite severely, was taken to San Francisco for treatment. Even the horses and the stage escaped with but very little injury. The stage and the two horses arrived in this city about twelve o'clock.

Marin Journal, 16 December 1909

Supervisor Michael Burke investigated the incident and exonerated the "deputy road inspector," Mr. M. S. Truet, who was in fact a deputy fish and game commissioner for the Fairfax district and not connected with the road.

"The road was condemned by the supervisors two years ago," said Burke, "and no one should be blamed for the condition of the bridge."

This was disingenuous at best, for many did blame the Board of Supervisors. They had abandoned the old road in March 1906 and three and a half years later the bypass was still not ready for use. The winter rains had arrived, and because the bypass had not yet been graveled, it was closed to vehicular traffic to avoid damage. Even though the old road was no longer maintained, the stagecoaches were forced to continue to use it. Supervisor Burke did have the bridge repaired though, and traffic was resumed.

By this time motor vehicles had become common. They were limited to four miles per hour when crossing bridges and were supposed to allow plenty of room to horses, but accidents occurred, including this one to Al's Dipsea Stage:

FOUR INJURED IN MISHAP ON MOUNTAIN ROAD
MILL VALLEY, Aug. 29— Four persons were injured yesterday afternoon, when the four-horse stagecoach running between West Point, on Mount Tamalpais, and Willow camp plunged over the roadside into Steep ravine, hurling the seven passengers and the driver 200 feet below among the trees and underbrush.

Alburto Bement, a prominent Chicago consulting engineer, and his young bride sustained the most serious hurts, Mrs. Bement receiving a broken nose and lacerations of the face, head, and arms, while her husband dislocated his right ankle and received minor injuries. Mrs. Gardner, wife of a physician of Willows, had two broken ribs as the result of one of the horses falling upon her. Her 7 year old daughter, Helen, was scratched and bruised and her leg cut, but not seriously. Three men who sat in the rear seat were injured.

MotorCyclists Scare Team

The horses became frightened at three motor cyclists, who were coasting down the grade toward the stage, which was a three-seated vehicle with a canopy top. Manuel Nunes, the driver, warned the cyclists to stop, but they gave no heed. The four horses reared backward, the leaders turning completely around in the narrow road. The rear horses followed, and in an instant horses, coach and passengers had pitched over the edge into the deep canyon.

The men in the rear seat jumped, but the driver and other passengers had no chance to escape. Bement and his wife sat in the middle seat, while Mrs. Gardner and the child sat with the driver. Mrs. Bement attempted to jump as the coach turned over, but fell, striking upon her face on the steep slope. Bement, Mrs. Gardner and the little girl rolled down with the leaders of the team, the horses struggling to free themselves from the harness. Trees and shrubbery blocked them from falling to the bottom of the ravine, but they rolled 200 feet before they were halted by a clump of redwoods.

San Francisco Call, 30 August 1910

By 1910 plans were under way to build a new dam at Alpine that would flood the entire Lagunitas Valley. In July 1910, foreseeing the impending loss of his property, Sam Pezzaglia gave up the Liberty Ranch:

> Mingled with pleasure and regrets his many friends will learn that S. Pezzaglia, the genial host of Liberty Ranch, has disposed of his place after eighteen years' incumbency, and will hereafter reside at San Anselmo. Mr. Pezzaglia would like to settle all matters connected with his business, but as he is unable to reach everybody personally he has adopted the *Journal* as the official means of notifying the public of this change, asking that all claims may be addressed to him at San Anselmo. While we are sorry to see Mr. Pezzaglia giving up the active management of the place which he has made popular, we are nevertheless glad to see him reap the fruits of his many years' toil.
>
> *Marin Journal*, 21 July 1910

So after more than thirty years of operation, Liberty's resort closed down. It was rented to the Lagunitas Rod and Gun Club, which used it as their clubhouse. The all-male club leased 12,000 acres of the mountain for their hunting and fishing pursuits.

In November, Al Sayers hired his son Willy, 18, who had been working as a clerk in a butcher shop:

> William Sayers is holding the ribbons on the Bolinas stage line. He expects to run through the winter.
>
> *Marin County Tocsin*, 26 November 1910

But after only three years, Albert Sayers sold the line again:

> BOLINAS STAGE LINE CHANGES OWNERS
> Albert Sayers, who for years has operated the Bolinas-San Rafael stage line, has sold the property to John Strain and W. H. McEvoy. The new proprietors are capable and popular business men and the line will undoubtedly continue to prosper.
>
> *Marin County Tocsin*, 12 August 1911

Albert Sayers bought the George Hudson ranch at Bolinas. He died there in 1921, aged sixty-one. His son William Albert Sayers died in San Francisco in 1960, aged sixty-eight.

The Strain-McEvoy Stagecoach, 1911-1913

John Strain was the man trapped in the stagecoach when the bridge collapsed in 1909. Two years later, he and his partner William H. McEvoy bought the line from Al Sayers. They had been running the stage just four months when another bad accident occurred:

WIFE OF NOTED SCIENTIST HURT IN A RUNAWAY
Mrs. Stratton, Pinned Down by Overturned Stage, May Lose Her Arm
Philosophy Professor, Who Was Also in the Vehicle, Is Severely Bruised

SAN RAFAEL, Dec. 2.—Mrs. George M. Stratton, wife of Professor Stratton, head of the department of philosophy of the University of California, was so seriously injured in a runaway accident on the Bolinas road late yesterday afternoon that amputation of her right arm may be necessary. Professor Stratton, who was with his wife at the time of the accident, was severely bruised, but none of his bones was broken. The team attached to a stage in which the couple were riding ran away at the Summit house at the top of the Bolinas ridge while the driver, George Farrell[43], was unloading freight and Stratton was holding the reins from his place on the back seat. The frightened team dashed down the steep stage road, the front wheels of the vehicle striking the bank at a sharp curve and the stage overturned. The horses did not stop in their mad career, but continued dragging the heavy wagon, in which the Strattons were imprisoned by the canvas top. For 50 yards the vehicle was dragged with its helpless occupants along the dizzy edge of the Canyon road. At any moment it might have turned over the edge of the road down the

---

[43] George Henry Farrell (1871-1932) was the brother of Mamie Farrell Sayers and brother-in-law of Albert Sayers. At this time he was living with the Sayers family.

ravine to the bottom 200 feet below. But the rear wheels struck the protruding trunk of a tree, which checked its course. The traces broke and the horses ran free. Farrell, the driver, followed the runaways on foot. When he reached the wagon he found that Mrs. Stratton was suffering from a compound fracture of the right arm, a simple fracture of the left wrist and bruises on her body and wrist. With the aid of W. Brown, caretaker at the Summit house, the injured persons were removed to that place. Farrell drove to Bolinas in a buggy and secured the automobile of William Sayers at that place, and the Strattons were taken to San Rafael in the car. Farrell's explanation of the cause of the accident is that his horses, which had been long in the service, must have become frightened at a caged fox that he was unloading from the stage. Professor Stratton, from his place in the rear of the stage, was unable to control the maddened animals once they had started, and Farrell, running at his top speed after the team, could not overtake it until its course was ended. The only damage done the stage was a broken spring. The stage horses escaped into the hills after the accident and had not been caught late this afternoon.

San Francisco Call, 3 December 1911

It was clearly time for the stages to modernize. But Strain and McEvoy knew nothing about automobiles. In September 1913, they sold the line to someone who did:

HISTORIC STAGE LINE TO BOLINAS EXPIRES

SAN RAFAEL, Sept. 25.—The famous old Bolinas stage line, which has been in existence for nearly half a century, will pass into history the first of October.

On that day the picturesque old bus, drawn by four horses, which has wound its way dally through the scenic beauty of the mountainous trip for so many years, will give way to two modern seven passenger automobiles.

San Francisco Call, 25 September 1913

So after 34 years of service, the big four-horse stages would no longer rumble over the Bolinas-Fairfax Road. For the generations who had grown up riding these stages, it was clear that an era of Marin history had passed.

The Crane-Langford Auto Coach, 1913-1916

The Stanley Mountain Wagon

Ernest Albert Langford was born in Canada in 1864. He came to this country as a teenager and married Grace Lily Williamson in 1891. They lived at 23 Olive Avenue in the Dominican neighborhood of San Rafael, a house that still stands. He was one of the first visionaries in Marin who saw the coming rise of the automobile. Around 1905, aged 41, he formed a partnership with Bud Crane, 45, to operate a livery for automobiles. That same year, he got one of the first moving violations in the county:

Last Friday E. A. Langford, a chauffeur operating the automobile of the Hotel Rafael, was dismissed by Justice Magee. He had been arrested for operating the auto in the night time without displaying the necessary light. On the trial, Mr. Langford and his witnesses testified that the lights were burning and that the rear one went out during the ride and that they were not aware of it.

Marin Journal, 31 August 1905

Tarleton Lee "Bud" Crane was born in Missouri in 1860. When he was four, he came to California with his parents in a mule caravan. In 1882 he married Mary Eleanor Wilkes (1863-1943). He worked as a conductor on the railroad until 1905, when the partners founded the first garage in Marin County.

Their first office was at 322 Fourth Street in San Rafael (now the site of Whole Foods) and functioned as the Automobile Livery, offering their services as chauffeurs and renting automobiles. Later they moved to 435 Fourth Street (corner of Grand Ave.) and started selling Packards and Dodges. In September 1913, they purchased the Bolinas-San Rafael Stage Line:

NEW AUTOMOBILE SERVICE TO BOLINAS

The historic old Bolinas stage line which has been plying between this city and Bolinas for 25 or more years is soon to be a thing of the past and horse flesh will give way to the fast automobile which will cut the time between this city and the seacoast from four hours to two. Messrs. Crane and Langford of the Auto Livery Company of this city have consummated a deal whereby they acquire the Bolinas stage company and its mail contracts and will take charge October 1st. It is their intention to put several Packard machines in the service and will make the trip in two hours. Under this new arrangement San Francisco mail reaching this city by 10 a. m., will be delivered at Bolinas at 12 M. of the same day.

Marin County Tocsin, 27 September 1913

In the end, the partners decided against using their own Packards and Dodges. Perhaps the steep mountain grades proved too much for the small engines of the early models. They opted for the more powerful Stanley Steamer Mountain Wagon, specifically designed for steep grades.

The Mountain Wagon had two vertical steam cylinders heated by burning gasoline, developing twelve horsepower. In 1906, a similar Stanley vehicle had set the mile speed record of 127 MPH.

The public was excited about being able to get to Bolinas so quickly in the beautiful new machines:

The New Bolinas Stage

Saturday, November 15th, the maiden trip of the new Stanley Mountain Wagon, owned by Crane & Langford, was made to Bolinas, covering the ground in about one hour and a half. This car is a great favorite mountain car, used for steep grades and can be relied upon as one that is equal to the heavy grades on the Bolinas road. Mr. Crane hopes in time to make arrangements with Uncle Sam in carrying the mails so as to be able to make the round trip to Bolinas in one day; as it is, the Bolinas traffic has more than doubled, carrying over three hundred passengers during the month of October; this is a great improvement on the old way of travelling, formerly taking nearly four hours to make the trip.

Marin Journal, 20 November 1913

The steamer stage arriving in Bolinas. Courtesy of the California Room at the Marin County Free Library

By 1915 Tarleton Crane was 55 and apparently needed a break:

LOCAL AUTO FIRM SEVERS INTERESTS

The desire of T. L. Crane to "rest a little" from his active labors of the past few years has led to a mutual agreement between himself and E. A. Langford, associated in the auto livery business for many years, to dissolve their co-partnership in the establishment at No. 435 Fourth Street.

Mr. Crane is to take sole charge of the Buick Automobile agency. Mr. Langford will conduct the Bolinas Stage Line, operating between San Rafael and Bolinas.

Marin Journal, 20 December 1915

So Bud Crane left the stage business. He retired in the 1920s and died in San Rafael in 1933, aged 73.

At the end of 1915, Langford made a major change in the route:

The Bolinas Stage is now running between Sausalito and Bolinas instead of out of San Rafael. Mr. E. A. Langford, a pioneer and a very careful automobile driver, has the contract for carrying the mail between Sausalito and Stinson's Beach and Bolinas, making one round trip each week day. The stage leaves here at nine a. m. and Bolinas at 12:45 p. m.

Sausalito News, 4 November 1916

After 37 years of continuous operation, there would be no more stages between San Rafael and Bolinas. San Rafael residents were not pleased, as a trip to Bolinas now included the time and expense of a train ticket to Sausalito:

BOLINAS STAGE HAS NEW TERMINUS

Beginning November 1st the Bolinas stage line will have its southern terminus at Sausalito. The mail contract for the new year has been awarded again to Mr. Langford, who will move his equipment to Sausalito, and hereafter it will be necessary for residents of San Rafael to take the Bolinas stage at that point. The stage will deliver mail both to Willow Camp and Bolinas over this route, thus obviating the necessity for two stage lines. The change of schedule will be felt by San Rafael merchants, who have in the past enjoyed the patronage of the Bolinas people who traveled via the line.

Marin Journal, 26 October 1916

Five years later, Langford sold the Sausalito-Bolinas line:

LANGFORD TO DISPOSE OF BOLINAS STAGE LINE

E. A. Langford, who has been operating for a number of years the stage line between Sausalito and Bolinas, via Stinson Beach, has negotiated for the sale of the business to W. H. Caltoft. Langford has asked the Railroad Commission for its approval of the sale. During the summer and fall months Langford has been operating five and six large stages to care for the vacationists at Stinson Beach and Bolinas.

Marin Journal, 29 September 1921

The sale was approved and closed October 6, and Langford and his wife took off on an auto tour of Southern California and Arizona. He started an automobile finance company in San Francisco. In 1924 they moved to Pasadena.

Walter H. Caltoft (1882-1941) was a cheesemaker and creamery manager from Petaluma. In 1912 he married Martha "Mattie" Foss (1876-1960). He ran the Sausalito-to-Bolinas stage for twenty more years, using a combination of Stanleys, Studebakers, a ten-passenger Packard, and a fleet of three White buses bought from Yosemite Park.

A Yosemite Transportation Company bus at the park, similar to those purchased by Walter Caltoft.

When Walter died in 1941, his wife Mattie continued to run the line in her station wagon. With the influx of workers to the Marinship shipyard in Sausalito during World War II, demand for public transport between Bolinas and Sausalito increased. Greyhound bought the line from Mrs. Caltoft and ran it throughout the war. At the end of the war, the service was discontinued.

After sixty-five years of service, there was no longer any stage to Bolinas. But the Bolinas-Fairfax was still in use by private and commercial vehicles and it remained a vital transportation and shipping link to Bolinas. It seemed a permanently fixed feature of the county.

There were more changes in store for it, however, and to tell that story we have to back up to the beginning of the twentieth century and examine the contentious issue that shaped most communities in the West—water.

Alpine Dam, 1908-1918

Alpine Dam under construction. Lagunitas bridge in foreground. Photo courtesy of MMWD.

The San Francisco earthquake and fire of April 1906 had left a quarter of a million people homeless in San Francisco—more than half the city's residents. The poor lived in vast tent cities. Many of the wealthy fled to their summer homes in Marin where they had long been accustomed to spending their holidays. They converted these summer cottages into permanent residences, everything from rustic cabins to mansions. Land was at a premium. The huge old ranchos and vast family estates were being subdivided. Houses were creeping up into the canyons of Mill Valley, Corte Madera, and Larkspur. San Rafael sprouted several major additions. John Orey Baptiste Short (1828-1902) and his brother Jacob (1834-1895) subdivided their large holdings to the south of the railroad tracks and called it Short's Addition. The Coleman Addition, developed by William Tell Coleman (1824-1893) went east into the current Dominican neighborhood.

Even sleepy backwaters like Kentfield, San Anselmo and Fairfax were lined with realtors' offices covered with signs advertising building lots. The good railroad and ferry system made commuting to the City practical. People flocked here. The population of Marin soared 20% in the first decade of the century.

With the burgeoning growth came a growing demand for water. Even with the completion of Phoenix Lake, supply was not keeping up with demand. Realtors couldn't sell houses where the water supply wasn't reliable. The county clearly needed another large reservoir.

In the spring of 1908 the Marin County Water Company reorganized as the Marin Water and Power Company and abandoned plans for the Tamalpais Dam. They proposed to do what the Shafter-Howard family's Lagunitas Water Company had proposed—build a much larger structure farther downstream at Alpine, where the Lagunitas Creek plunged into a steep gorge. A dam in that narrow canyon would be on solid rock and could be built much taller and form a larger reservoir.

But this proposal raised many issues. First, of course, the site and much of the surrounding watershed was owned by the Shafter-Howards, who wanted to build and own the dam themselves. The company claimed that the family had already granted them an easement back in 1871, but the family said they had never intended to give up the valuable water rights to their land. Acquiring the land would require legal action.

Second, the resulting reservoir would submerge much of the Lagunitas Valley, and a number of people lived there. In addition to the commercial operations of Liberty Ranch, the Lagunitas Rod and Gun Club, and Jory's Redwood Inn, there were also numerous private cabins along the creek. Most of these were leases from the Shafter-Howards. George H. Jackson, Vice-President of the gun club, had taken over the old Kent place, demolished the old ruined cabin, and built a small house and stable. Just the year before he had built a house, barn, bridge, keeper's house, corral and fencing. One cabin belonged to the prominent dentist Edgar R. R. Parker, who advertised statewide and had legally changed his name to Painless Parker. Others were leased by the Scotts, Jacksons, Crosbys, Crooks, and Miss Alice Hoffman. Some of these places had started as rustic cabins but had been improved over the years into attractive homes. These people, many of them wealthy and powerful, objected strongly to having their homes and ranches flooded.

Third, the new lake would inundate a large portion of the Bolinas-Fairfax road, threatening to isolate Bolinas again.

Law suits were filed, and the water users of Marin waited while the various cases ground through the courts. In the case of Jory's Redwood Inn, the jury voted in February 1908 to condemn the right of way and awarded the family $2,900 instead of the $50,000 they had demanded. William Jory threatened to appeal the decision, though he later conceded his defeat. But the Shafter-Howard family continued their lawsuit, and there was little progress toward constructing the dam.

As the dry winter continued and the water in the reservoirs continued to fall, there was increasing public pressure to find a solution. When no compromise could be reached, a number of alternative routes were proposed. One was from the town of Lagunitas up the Lagunitas Canyon (now Kent Lake) to Alpine. Another would run from Mill Valley to West Point (roughly the Hoo-koo-e-koo Road and trail today). The latter was of course greatly favored by Mill Valley residents and businessmen. Although the road from West Point to Willow Camp was a private road built and owned by Sydney Cushing of the Scenic Railway, it was thought that he was public-spirited enough to donate the road to the County. If either of these roads were to be built, it would render the Bolinas-Fairfax road obsolete.

The third option was a bypass recommended by the road viewers that would cut off from the Bolinas-Fairfax just east of Liberty's, climb up Liberty Gulch, then double back up Azalea hill, to reconnect with the Bolinas-Fairfax near Jory's gate.

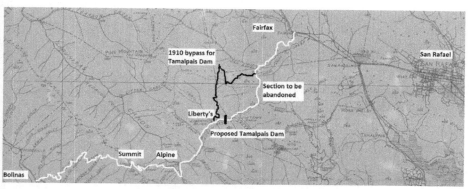

Third Option: The Liberty bypass across the Jory place

In the end, the board approved this third choice. They requested bids to build the bypass. On August 3rd they awarded a contract for $11,800 to the firm of Wilkins and Redding. This was James Hepburn Wilkins who with Jesse Colwell, had built the original road more than thirty years earlier. After decades supervising the state prison system, at age 55 he had returned to building roads. His partner was Charles Augustus Redding, 37, of Nicasio, who had worked as an armorer at San Quentin. Their new partnership had secured several lucrative contracts for graveling and paving San Rafael city streets. They rented the Jory ranch as the headquarters for the project.

Work started August 30th, 1909. By November, they had made enough progress that the Grand Jury came out to inspect the work:

Grand Jurymen Stalled in Hills

While on a tour of inspection over the new and completed portion of the Fairfax-Bolinas road yesterday morning, the Grand Jury committee, consisting of J. Fred Schlingman of Mill Valley, Q. Codoni of Tocaloma, M. Herzog of San Rafael and County Surveyor Richardson became stalled on the road through the Jory ranch. One of the axles of their rig went dry and the wheel stuck. The party alighted and ornamented tree stumps with their persons, until a monkey-wrench and some axle grease could be procured from Jory's. After this the party continued the trip.

Marin County Tocsin, 13 November 1909

Liberty Gulch Road emerging from Alpine Lake. The foundations of Liberty Ranch are under the water to the left.

It was March 1910 before the new Liberty Gulch road was complete. But rains that season made the road impassible until a layer of gravel could be applied.

The people of Marin were becoming increasingly frustrated with the endless haggling between the rival water companies. Many people considered their water rates excessive. As early as 1894, a Tax Reform League was formed, with one of their objectives the establishment of a publicly-owned water district. That had never been done before in California and there was no legal precedent. For a public entity to condemn the lands and assets of a private company, fair compensation would have to be paid, and there was great disagreement in setting a monetary value on watersheds. Arguments continued in the papers and supervisors' meetings, but public opinion, and especially the *Marin Journal*, were strongly arguing that something had to change.

In 1910, George Harlan of Sausalito was elected to the State Assembly. A strong supporter of a water district, he promptly submitted a bill called the Water District Act. Under the Act, two thirds of the affected voters could approve the creation of a municipal water district, supported by local taxes or bond issues, and having broad power to seize land by eminent domain. The Act set forth procedures for determining the fair market value of any property to be seized.

The bill passed in May 1911 and was signed into law. The Marin County supervisors scheduled a special election to form such a district in southern and central Marin. It would incorporate the lands and assets of both the Marin Water and Power Company (serving San Rafael, San Anselmo, Larkspur, Sausalito, San Quentin, and Angel Island) and the North Coast Water Company (serving Mill Valley and Belvedere). The election was postponed until April 13, 1912, to give the newly-enfranchised women time to register to vote. In this election, the first in which Marin women participated, voters approved by an 85% majority the creation of the Marin Municipal Water District (MMWD). People celebrated the victory. For the first time, the water supply would be controlled by a single locally-elected board, answerable to the people, and rates would be standardized. There was talk of making the entire watershed a public park for the enjoyment of all, rather than a series of private leaseholds.

The only people not celebrating were the existing water companies. Worrying that any money spent in improving their facilities might not be recovered in the settlement, they canceled any planned improvements and even deferred routine maintenance. Service became unreliable and there were several serious water supply breakdowns. After a year of studies, the MMWD set the value of both companies at three million dollars (about $72 million today), which was generally thought fair. They proposed a bond issue to raise the funds.

The Water District invited all interested persons to a "basket picnic" at the site of the proposed Alpine Dam on May 31, 1915. Hundreds attended, though there were not enough automobiles for the crowd that gathered at the Fairfax railroad station. Perhaps the Bolinas Stage helped to ferry them to the site. Congressman William Kent[44] spoke at the picnic:

"It so happened that about thirty-five years back my father became the possessor of three hundred and five shares of the capital stock of the old Marin County Water Company. Precisely what has happened to that stock in the intervening years I have no means of finding out, but at any rate that stock represents a very definite proportion of the property of the Marin Water & Power Company.

"That stock has paid six per cent ever since I have known anything about it: that property has been practically a protected monopoly, and the people in their water rates have paid it. I feel that I have had enough out of that property and I am going to put the stock in trust to be given to the District in the event of the bonds passing. That will be a little help.

"In regard to the Park matter, it so happens that I am possessed of some land on the other side of the watershed and a little, a very little, on this slope. I intend to make a present of a considerable number of acres, not a very vast tract, but enough so that the right to travel along that ridge and to see the ocean, in so far as my land lies, shall be preserved to the public, and I hope to be able in other ways to aid in piecing out that park."

Marin County Tocsin, 5 June 1915

This was no small offer. His stock was worth over a million in today's dollars, and his donation of Bolinas Ridge and much of Mount Tamalpais ensured these lands would be preserved. His gifts later led to the creation of Mount Tamalpais State Park. He is also the man

---

[44] William Kent was born in Chicago in 1864. His father A. E. Kent moved the family to Marin in 1871, where he bought an 800-acre estate that is now Kentfield. William Kent was elected to the US Congress from 1911 to 1917. He died in 1928.

responsible for saving Muir Woods, so Marin residents have a lot to thank him for.

This picnic was a seminal event in the creation of the public watershed. The event was very successful and people were favorably impressed with the District's plans. An unnamed filmmaker shot a thousand feet of film of the historic picnic but, sadly, the film has never been found.

On August 28, the bond issue passed overwhelmingly by more than three to one. The bonds were issued and sold quickly. The District purchased the necessary Shafter-Howard land for $137,000 and took over the assets of the Marin Power and Water Company and the North Coast Water Company. The companies were dissolved, and shareholders received checks for $80 per share. Most were very happy with the deal, as the stock had never traded over $65.

The District hired civil engineer Albert Read Baker (1882-1936) to design the project. He was born in Norwalk Ohio, raised in San Diego, and studied civil engineering at Berkeley. In 1913, he married Ivy Grace Hayward (1889-1981) and they had four children. Though only thirty years old—the papers called him "the boy engineer"—he would prove a very competent engineer for the project.

In addition to the dam, the project required a massive system to transport the water to San Rafael. This included building a 2-mile pipeline down the gorge below the dam (under the Alpine-Kent Pump Road), a tunnel 1.7 miles long under the Pine Mountain Ridge toward Fairfax (the tunnel still exists but is used only for water storage), and a pipeline and tunnel from there 4.4 miles to Phoenix Lake (under Pine Mountain Tunnel Road and Concrete Pipe Road). From there, the water would be pumped through new cast-iron pressure pipelines five miles to San Rafael and four miles to Mill Valley. All these projects were to begin immediately, while the design of the dam was finalized and the site cleared.

In the fall of 1916, as war raged in Europe, construction finally began. F. C. Peters, who had built a lovely rustic homestead near the Lagunitas Bridge, sold his cabin to the District to serve as the construction headquarters.

On the first of November, 1916, the last lawsuits were settled and the District took official possession of the lands of both water companies and all the affected landowners and tenants. A work crew consisting of a foreman, a cook, and ten laborers was assigned to begin clearing the site of the dam. They cleared the trees and exposed bedrock on both sides of the canyon from the streambed up 170 feet to the projected elevation of the top of the dam. Soon crews were using diamond bits to drive test bores into the rock.

A new contract was awarded to S. P. Brownlee to improve the Bolinas-Fairfax Road between Summit and Bolinas:

> The Bolinas grade job consists of about four miles of regrading, and calls for the widening, straightening some curves, and reducing the grades, so that the new road will be 16 feet wide with a width of 20 feet on the curves, and the steepest grade will be 9½ per cent and this may be reduced to 7½ per cent. The work starts at the top of the grade and extends down the westerly slopes to near Bolinas bay. The contract price is $9,435.30.

Marin Journal, 7 December 1916

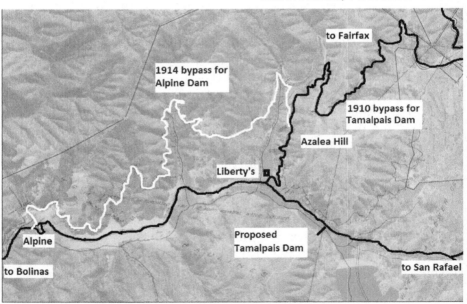

The proposed changes marked on a 1914 MMWD map, overlain on a modern map

The new reservoir would flood the Lagunitas valley from Alpine to Bontempi, up to a hundred feet deep, flooding yet another section of the Bolinas-Fairfax. A survey crew arrived to begin the work of laying out the new bypass around the reservoir. They lived first in the Hoffman cottage, then moved to the Jackson house, as the hills were stripped of their trees and soil.

Congressman Kent proposed that the Bolinas-Fairfax Road be moved to the other side of the valley, running from Phoenix Lake across the lower knees of Tamalpais to Alpine, saying the views and grades would be better. His plan was not adopted, probably because it would eliminate access between Bolinas and Fairfax.

The surveyors proposed that the new road run across the top of the dam from the west bank of Cataract Creek, eliminating the bridges across both Lagunitas and Cataract Creeks. On the north side, it would contour through the redwoods across the steep slopes, gradually climbing until it struck the Liberty Gulch Road well above the level of the doomed Liberty's.

Raising the Bolinas-Fairfax Road in 1917 for Alpine Dam. Photo courtesy of MMWD.

In February 1917, the contract to build the Pine Mountain Tunnel was let to McLaren and Peterson for $257,500. A. J. Fairbanks got the contract to build the replacement for the Bolinas-Fairfax for $22,761. He also won the contract to clear 135 acres of the valley to be flooded. The buildings of the old Liberty Ranch were razed and carted away, along with all the other houses, barns, and other structures in the valley. Thousands of trees were cut and hauled to mills.

On May 26, the District approved the final plans for the dam and advertised for bids. The engineers reported that the new road was about

163

one quarter complete and on schedule, but the tunnel was running late. When the contractors were asked to explain, they had an unusual excuse:

McLaren and Petersen, who have charge of the tunnel contract, having been criticized to some extent for delays in their work, stated in a letter that the reason for this was the readiness of the saloons in Fairfax to keep the tunnel employees supplied with liquor, even to the extent of sending consignments out to the job. They urged that the matter be taken up with the Supervisors to see if some curb could be placed on the custom as it affected the Water District laborers.

Marin Journal, 14 June 1917

Finally, on Saturday, September 22, 1917, the directors of the District drove out to the dam site to watch the big mixing machines start pouring concrete. Nine years after it was first proposed, the dam began to rise.

Alpine Dam under construction. Note the trees cleared to the projected waterline. Bolinas Ridge beyond. Photo courtesy MMWD.

But in October union laborers, many of them Greek immigrants, walked off the job, followed by a dozen non-union men. The teamsters quit as well, offered better pay by a trucking firm. In January 1918, the contractors said they could not fulfill the contract and the District took over the work. Work continued throughout the year. By December 7th the new road was finished, and the tunnel, pipelines, and dam were completed on December 19th, 1918.

Marin had a lot to celebrate. The huge new dam was complete and the lake started filling with the winter rains. Water began running through the new 20-mile-long gravity system. There would be enough water for the foreseeable future. The rerouted and improved Bolinas-Fairfax road was again open for travel. And just a month earlier, the Great War had ended.

Major storms in January 1921 sent huge amounts of water through the spillways:

The spillways of the Alpine Dam in the recent storm carried away 900,000,000 gallons of water, almost enough to fill the great reservoir built by "The Boy Engineer," and which it was predicted at one time would hold more than the watershed could furnish in a whole season.

Marin Journal, 20 January 1921

Although no lives had been lost in the big construction project, there was one fatality as the bulkheads were being removed. It was Dave McCurdy, younger brother of Hugh McCurdy who had owned the stagecoach line:

David McCurdy Dies in Tragic Accident

Victim of a tragic accident, David McCurdy, employed by the Marin Municipal Water District, met death last Saturday at Alpine Dam above Fairfax while removing some heavy timbers used as a bunker during the construction work on the dam.

McCurdy was in charge of a gang of men and was attempting to loosen one of the timbers from the bank so that it could be drawn away by an auto truck. One end of the timber gave way suddenly and swung, striking McCurdy on the back of the head. Death was instantaneous.

He had been employed at Alpine Lake for some time and held a responsible position. He comes of a highly respected and pioneer Marin county family. For many years in his early youth he resided with father and mother, brothers and sisters in Bolinas.

Marin Journal, 14 April 1921

Almost immediately, people began illegally swimming in the new lake. On the same day in May—no doubt a warm spring day—there were two separate arrests:

> Judge de la Montanya of San Rafael fined T. Langes of San Francisco $50 on charge of polluting the waters of Alpine Lake. Mr. [William H.] Stein, keeper of the Alpine Dam Property, administered the arrest.
>
> Again the water of Alpine dam has been used for other than drinking purposes. This time the Misses Beth Smithson and Enid Remick were having a wonderful time wading in it, right in the shadow of a large sign advising the public as to just what the water was for. However they were apprehended by Officer Stein who took them to San Rafael and brought them before Justice of the Peace Montanya by whom they were fined $25 each.
>
> *Sausalito News*, 19 May 1923

The perpetrators were Enid Lenore Remick (1902-1955) and Elizabeth Maud Smithson (1903-1988) of San Rafael, 20-year-old coeds at Berkeley. A $25 fine was equivalent to $350 today, so the two young ladies paid dearly for wading. Mr. Langes was fined twice as much, so perhaps he did more than wade, or maybe he just wasn't as pretty.

In 1924, the California and Hawaiian Sugar Company (C&H) needed much more water for its refinery in Crockett and contracted with the Water District to supply it. To meet this new demand, the Water District raised Alpine Dam by eight feet, increasing the storage of the lake from three thousand acre-feet to four thousand. A new 12" pipeline called the Sugar Line was built six miles to C&H's pier at San Quentin (now the Marin Rod and Gun Club pier), where they picked it up in water barges to haul to their refinery. The project cost $59,000, paid entirely by C&H. The Bolinas-Fairfax road was closed from June to October 1924 while the construction was going on.

After the Dam, 1919-1936

Even before the dam, the scenic beauty of the Bolinas-Fairfax had attracted one of Marin's newest industries, film-making. In 1911 the California Motion Picture Company built a large studio in San Rafael and turned out more than two hundred films, nearly all westerns starring "Broncho Billy" Anderson, one of the owners of the company.

A still from the 1914 hit "Salomy Jane," showing a stagecoach barreling down the Fairfax Grade with Tamalpais in the background.

The same spot a century later. Photos courtesy of Joe Breeze.

Odd stories continued to arise from the Bolinas-Fairfax:

LEFT ON BOLINAS RIDGE IN RAGING STORM, MAN IS SAVED BY PASSING AUTO PARTY

Atop the bleak Bolinas Ridge,
A shivering traveler stood.
The night was dark, the fog was thick;
Storm gods in a terrible mood.

That was the setting one awful night last week for a little playlet that might be called "The Good Samaritan of Bolinas Ridge." A belated party of three men were threading their way in an auto along the precipitous cliffs of the ridge from Bolinas to San Rafael. Darkness, fog, rain and wind coalesced with the foul purpose of destroying any and all venturesome mites with temerity enough to invade the playground of Jupiter Pluvius[45].

Suddenly, as in all thrilling stories, something happened. A piercing yell split the night into three or four pieces of irregular dimensions. The machine rounded a steep bluff, and ahead, through one of the fissures caused by the yell, the occupants of the machine saw a figure clinging to the steep bluff on the inside of the road. Pinioned as it were, by the glare of the headlight to the dripping cliff, the figure waved hands and feet in wild gesticulation, at the same time emitting further incoherence.

The machine passed him and then stopped. Like an avalanche the figure catapulted down the grade. The occupants of the car had some misgivings. The man might have a gun and sinister designs. He might have strabismus[46] of the brain and great bodily strength.

Be that as it might, however, he catapulted against the car and into the glare of the headlight. He had wild eyes, no hat and incoherence of speech. The flood of English words finally subsided to this:

"Oh, gee whiz, is that you George Merk? Oh, gee whiz, I'm tickled. Oh, gee!"

"Why, is that you, George Farrell?" asked Merk as he shut off the throb of his motor.

---

[45] The Roman god of rain.
[46] Strabismus means misalignment of the eyes. Probably used in error.

"Yes, it's me! Oh, gee, I'm glad. I was just fixin' to stay all night. Al Sayers drove off and left me, and I lost my hat, and everything, and I was fixin' to stay all night, and everything, and I'm cold, and everything, and oh, gee, I'm glad you come."

The auto party passed Sayers four miles above where Farrell shivered hatless and deserted in the fog and wind and rain.

Farrell, at the invitation of George Merk, who was the Good Samaritan in the playlet, climbed into the machine and was whirled away to a warm bed in San Rafael.

Marin Journal, 16 December 1915

There is no indication why Albert Sayers, the former stagecoach owner, should have abandoned his unfortunate brother-in-law on the mountain in a storm.

Here's another tale from January 1919:

Hearse No Terror for This Man

If you and your wife were riding on a motorcycle way out in the country, and the said cycle should suddenly become refractory, buck, throw you off and insist upon lying in the ditch, and a hearse should appear on the bleak and lonely horizon, the only vehicle likely to show up for a half a day, and with room for but one on the seat, would you let your wife ride on the seat and walk home yourself, or would you ride inside? That is what a Baltimore Park man did last Saturday. He climbed right into the gruesome carriage and peered out through the frosted glass while the machine juggled over the ruts clear from the Alpine Dam down to Fairfax. Walter Castro and Manuel Azevedo were driving the vehicle back from Bolinas when they overtook the unfortunate couple. With room for but one more beside them on the seat, they offered a ride, and it was accepted, the gallant husband seating the lady properly and then taking his place in the interior.

Marin Journal, 16 January 1919

That year there was sad news of Mary Jane Liberty, the genial hostess and acclaimed cook:

DEATH OF MRS. LIBERTY OF LIBERTY RANCH

Word has been received here of the death on August 27th of Mrs. M. J. Liberty, in San Jose. The information will be a sad reminder to many of San Rafael's older citizens of the pleasant times in the past they enjoyed at "Liberty's," the old ranch that was famous about 20 years ago for the hospitality of its proprietors, who conducted a summer resort there. The site of the house now is submerged in the Alpine Lake, of the Municipal Water District, and nothing remains to indicate that at one time it was a gathering place for happy parties from all round the bay section.

Marin Journal, 11 September 1919

The winter rains that filled Alpine Lake so quickly in February were not good for the Bolinas-Fairfax:

The road recently built by the Marin Municipal Water District in place of the old road that ran through the Alpine dam site has been closed to "navigation" as it is a sea of mud. The water district directors requested the Board of Supervisors to have the county take this road over, but the Supervisors refused as the road was not up to requirements.

Mill Valley Record, 8 February 1919

It would not be the last time that the unpaved road would be damaged by winter storms. Washouts and landslides were common, and the road was sometimes closed for months. The County claimed that the District was responsible for its deteriorating condition. The District replied that they had built the road to the County's specifications at their own expense and tendered it to the County two years earlier, but the County had never accepted or maintained it. They said it was the County's responsibility and it would be illegal for the District to maintain a public road. Finally in December 1920 the County reluctantly accepted the road:

COUNTY ACCEPTS FAIRFAX ROAD

"Whereas, the Board of Supervisors ever mindful of the best interests of the traveling public and mindful of their duties have after all efforts to have the Marin Municipal Water District fulfill their public duties have determined in the interest of the public to expend the county money (to which the Water District do not contribute one dollar in taxes although it

170

is the principal user of the road) and put the road in passable condition at a cost estimated at three thousand dollars."

Marin Journal, 16 December 1920

In August 1923, the Supervisors let a contract to J. P. Holland to improve the road between Alpine and Bon Tempe[47] Meadows. He completed the work in December, but Lucy Jory asked the County to reimburse her for the construction of a bulkhead to protect her house, saying the bank had been made unstable by blasting for the road improvements. The Board denied her claim. By June 1924 the road was paved from San Rafael to Fairfax, oiled to Alpine Dam, and "fair graveled" to Bolinas.

In 1925, plans were announced to build a golf course on the Bolinas-Fairfax, today's Meadow Club:

Water District to Build Golf Course near Bon Tempe
The Marin Municipal Water District is considering leasing a 150 acre tract of land near Bon Tempe Meadows to be laid out for an eighteen-hole golf course. At a meeting of its directors last Tuesday night Messrs. Fisher and Rust, representing an Oakland concern, appeared before the board and put the proposition of a fifty-year lease of the large flat around the old Bon Tempe dam site, before the members. The board appointed a committee to view the tract and the committee will go over the ground today and report at the next regular meeting of the board.

Sausalito News, 24 January 1925

That same year, a major bond issue for $1,250,000 was passed to perform road improvements throughout the county. $82,250 of the funds were earmarked for the Bolinas-Fairfax. The road was closed and improvements started in March 1926. The job was finished in September, and almost fifty years after it was built, the Bolinas-Fairfax was still getting great reviews:

The road via the Alpine Lakes has been extensively improved and is now in excellent condition, having been graded, graveled and widened. This is a beautiful stretch of road as it winds through the Marin foothills, up

---

[47] The spelling changed from Bontempi to Bon Tempe sometime between 1902 and 1913.

hill and down dale, and for a considerable distance follows the shoreline of the Alpine Lakes, thence crosses the dam which forms the lakes. From this point there is a gradual and easy ascent to the beginning of the Ridgecrest Boulevard.

Sausalito News, 11 September 1926

In May 1927, there was a bad accident on the road:

CAR, 4 PEOPLE ROLL DOWN MOUNTAIN SIDE

Skidding from the road above the Alpine dam on Sunday afternoon, an automobile in which four San Francisco people were riding plunged over the bank at the side of the road and rolled more than 100 feet down the side of the mountain. Despite the fact that the car was reduced to a mass of wreckage, all the occupants escaped with minor cuts and bruises.

Those in the car at the time of the accident were Joseph Victor of 363 Tenth avenue and Ethel Victor, his wife, Alvin Philander and his wife, Mrs. Marian Philander, of the same address. After their injuries had been dressed at the Cottage hospital all were able to return to their homes in San Francisco.

According to Mrs. Victor, who was driving the car, the rear wheels of the machine skidded as she was making a turn.

As the heavy sedan rolled over and over the breaking glass cut all of the occupants of the machine, but the doors held and none were thrown from the car.

More than a score of motorists making the mountain climb witnessed the accident. Constable E. H. Horstkotter of San Rafael obtained their assistance and rushed the quartet to the hospital for treatment.

Sausalito News, 7 May 1927

In 1932, another project widened the road to 24 feet and re-graveled it, but it was later found that William L. Deysher, long the Chairman of the Board of Supervisors, had profited illegally by using his company's equipment on the project. After three trials, he was convicted of a felony and removed from the Board.

In 1934, the Civil Works Administration, a Depression-era program to find work for unemployed men, performed another major maintenance project. Eighty men widened and re-aligned portions of the road.

172

A major slide between Alpine and Summit closed the road in the storms of February 1936. Another repair project occurred in 1939.

The dams and the storms had a large impact on the Bolinas-Fairfax, but it was another mountain road that resulted in a huge upsurge in traffic. But for that story we have to again back up a few years.

Ridgecrest Boulevard, 1921-1925

Ridgecrest Boulevard heading up from the Bolinas-Fairfax Road toward Rock Spring.

By the 1920s, with most people now traveling by automobile, demand started to grow for a good safe road to the top of Mount Tamalpais. The old Eldridge Grade had been closed to vehicles fifteen years earlier and was no longer maintained. In 1921, Supervisor William Barr proposed that the County accept the grade and pave it for automobile use. Former congressman William Kent, who had donated most of the mountain to the public, objected:

Ex-Congressman William Kent, in discussing the Eldridge grade proposition recently said: "I am not in favor of opening up the Eldridge grade for the reason that it will disfigure the mountain on this side. Let us build a road from the summit of the Bolinas ridge at an altitude of 1500 feet around to Rock Springs, where an elevation of 2000 feet is attained. It would make the most wonderful drive in the world and the cost of this road would be very small."

Sausalito News, 2 July 1921

On August 18, 1921, the Board of Supervisors followed Congressman Kent's advice and voted to abandon the Eldridge Grade. In March 1922 the Water District voted to permit a new road to the summit:

The Water District Board assembled Tuesday evening gave its sanction to the proposed highway, which will traverse the lands of the district. Beginning at Ross the road past Alpine Dam would be included, thence up Ridgecrest to Bolinas Ridge, traversing this past Rock Spring, the road would climb West Peak and thence descend, by way of a portion of the old Eldridge Grade, to Tavern Tamalpais. This would make it possible for automobiles to reach the summit of the mountain by a gradual ascent. The proposition is to make this a toll road to provide for the payment and upkeep of it. H. C. Symonds, president of the Water District, says that in all probability this road and the proposed highway to Stinson Beach by way of Mill Valley will be constructed about the same time, the two

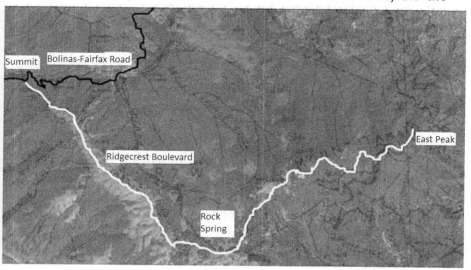

Ridgecrest Boulevard from the Bolinas-Fairfax Road to East Peak

connecting below Rock Spring. It may be necessary to provide for both highways by means of tolls.

Mill Valley Record, 25 March 1922

Under the auspices of the San Rafael and San Anselmo Chambers of Commerce, the Mount Tamalpais Ridgecrest Boulevard Company was formed. Stock was sold at $100 a share. The Water District bought some, as did the Scenic Railway. Engineers and attorneys were hired, and construction was started almost immediately, beginning at the site of the old Summit House. By November, the crews had reached Rock Spring:

Our Mountain Scenic Boulevard

The days of choosing between the alternatives of the hiker's enterprise or a trip of three transfers will pass into the limbo of things-that-were with the completion of the Mt. Tamalpais-Ridgecrest Boulevard, which already winds its smooth length from the middle of the summit of Bolinas Ridge to a point somewhat beyond Rock Spring. The workers now await wet weather and the opportunity to burn away the obstructing brush which keeps them from their goal.

The road is virtually a continuation of the well-known Fairfax-Bolinas road which winds above the Alpine Dam and circles down the western slope of Bolinas Ridge. The new route shunts off from the old highway at the crest of the ridge and undulates over the golden domes of Marin to Rock Spring; thence to West Peak, the present terminus, and when completed will extend to Middle Peak and thence to the door of the Tavern. At no point is the roadway narrower than twenty-four feet, while at the turns the width approaches forty feet. Every foot of the surface is exposed to the sun, thus insuring rapid drying after wet weather. The total cost of the road will reach $100,000, and the highway will be operated upon a toll basis, the revenues to be devoted to maintenance and to the reimbursement of stockholders.

Mill Valley Record, 18 November 1922

There must have been delays, for it was three more years before the road was completed:

MT. TAMALPAIS HIGHWAY OPEN TO MOTORISTS

Opened today, the Ridgecrest Boulevard to the top of Mt. Tamalpais is declared to offer scenery unparalleled in this section of the state. From the summit of towering Tamalpais it is possible to see the California coast line from Bodega Head nearly to Half Moon Bay and from Mt. Diablo to the Farallones, while in clear weather the Sierra Nevada Mountains may also be seen.

The Ridgecrest Boulevard was started about three years ago by the Central Marin Chamber of Commerce when a meeting was held at the Mt. Tamalpais Tavern and those present were so impressed by the wonderful night scenery that they decided an automobile road open day or night would be one of the greatest attractions Marin County could offer.

In a few days a subscription was started to start the organization of a company to begin the construction of a toll road. Those who formed the company were M. H. Ballou of San Anselmo, Thomas Kent of Kentfield, William Deysher, at that time a San Anselmo trustee and now Supervisor for the Second District in Marin county, Thomas P. Boyd, San Rafael attorney, and Fred Dickson.

The boulevard, which was formally opened yesterday, was largely financed by popular subscription.

"The views offered by the Ridgecrest Boulevard are absolutely unique in California highways," said Thomas Kent yesterday. "Running as it does on the backbone of the highest ridge in this part of the state, it allows the autoist to see the bay on the east and the ocean on the west in a number of places merely by turning his head.

"The round trip from Sausalito to the top of Mt. Tamalpais can easily be made in four hours. Another advantage it offers is that it isn't necessary to return to Sausalito on the same road as the run to Tamalpais was made.

"Leaving the ferry at Sausalito the motorist follows the Redwood Highway to San Anselmo and then turns left toward Fairfax. At the railroad tracks another left turn must be made to reach Bolinas avenue. Thence the route leads to the summit of Bolinas Ridge, past the beautiful Alpine Dam and the Marin Municipal Water District Park.

"Toll road starts at the summit of the Ridge and runs along the backbone of Tamalpais for about 7 miles at an average elevation of 2000 feet. The boulevard is rock surfaced, about 21 feet wide with ample width on all sides, and has a maximum grade of about 13 per cent.

"Returning to Sausalito and San Francisco instead of following the same route, turn to the left at the lower end of the toll road and drive to the north end of Bolinas Bay. Turn left again and follow the main road along Bolinas Bay through Stinson Beach to the Redwood Highway at Manzanita, and thence to Sausalito.

"In my opinion the new Ridgecrest Boulevard offers something unique in motoring, particularly in Northern California. A number of automobilists have already availed themselves of its advantages and all of them are quite enthusiastic about it.

"The Mt. Tamalpais Tavern has first class accommodations and meals are served any time of the day."

Sausalito News, 12 September 1925

The California State Automobile Association immediately trumpeted the beauties of the new road:

Toll Road up Mt. Tamalpais in good Condition Now

Motorists who want to make the trip to the summit of Mt. Tamalpais over the newly opened toll road will find the route in good condition, the touring bureau of the California State Automobile Association announced today. It is a wide highway and there are only a few places where it is necessary for some cars to use low gear.

The Automobile Association's scout car which covered the route last week reported that the road from Fairfax to Alpine dam is in good condition although it is a little narrow in places. The toll gate is located at the summit of the road between Alpine dam and Bolinas.

The distance from the toll gate to Tamalpais Tavern is approximately eight miles. Toll charges are $1 for the car and two passengers and 25 cents each for additional passenger.

Healdsburg Tribune, 24 October 1925

Ridgecrest remained a private toll road for the next fifteen years. In 1941, a movement was begun to have the State take it over:

Marin Senator Sponsors Ridgecrest Purchase

New steps were taken today in the move for state ownership of the Mt. Tamalpais Ridgecrest Boulevard in Marin County when the California Senate adopted a bill, sponsored by Senator Thomas F. Keating of San Rafael, which instructs the State Department of Public Works to investigate the advisability of state acquisition of the toll road. This act would require a survey to be made by the highway department and to be completed by July 1, 1942, so that the next session of the Legislature may have all of the facts upon which to act.

Sausalito News, 22 May 1941

Toll gate east of Summit. Courtesy of the Jack Mason Museum of West Marin History.

But these studies were derailed by the entry of the country into World War II a few months later. The Army saw Mount Tamalpais as a strategic site for military installations and took control of large parts of the mountain. Though the Ridgecrest Company owners might have lost income, the "autoists" gained:

No Toll on Mt. Drive 'Til Army Takes Over
Motorists may drive to the summit of Mt. Tamalpais without paying toll for the first time in modern history until the Army bans all traffic to that point. The Army instituted friendly suit in Federal court this week to take over the toll road rights and adjacent acreage from the Mount

179

Tamalpais Ridgecrest Boulevard company "for the duration" on a year-to-year lease basis. William Kent, Jr., president of the company, with the filing of the suit, dismissed the toll collectors and removed the toll gates at the panoramic highway junction.

Sausalito News, 16 July 1942

The following year a bill was passed to have the State Parks Department buy the road and adjoining lands for $90,000, but for undisclosed reasons, the bill was vetoed by Governor Earl Warren.

Following the war, the State Parks Department again tried to purchase Ridgecrest Boulevard. As part of the deal, the Water District offered a no-cost lease of East Peak as a recreation area. But the Attorney General determined that the lease had to include an option to buy, which the District was unwilling to grant, and the deal fell through.

It was not until July 1948 that State Parks purchased Ridgecrest Boulevard from the heirs of the Kent estate for $90,000, and also purchased 25 acres on East Peak, including the Tamalpais Tavern, for $25,000. Finally, Ridgecrest Boulevard was part of Mount Tamalpais State Park and permanently protected.

Raising the Dam, 1938-1942

The winter of 1938-9 was unusually dry, drawing Alpine Lake down to unprecedented levels. The District announced plans to raise Alpine Dam another thirty feet, more than doubling the capacity of the lake to nearly three billion gallons.

Alpine Dam before raising. Courtesy of MMWD.

This was a major project that cost $728,000. The contract went to Engineering Ltd. of San Francisco in August 1940. The road was closed to traffic in September, so that thousands of trees around the shore of the lake could be removed. The road approaches to the dam also had to be redesigned.

ALPINE DAM

Raising of Alpine Dam 30 feet to double Marin's water supply will soon be under way on a day and night schedule now that the end of the winter rains is in sight. Two shifts of men will be engaged in rushing the mixing and pouring of the thousands of yards of rock, sand and cement for the giant wall. There are 75 men now employed on the project, according to General Manager James S. Peters.

Sausalito News, 24 April 1941

New Technique Used on Alpine Dam

Raising of the Alpine Dam, Sausalito's and Marin County's principal water supply reservoir located between Fairfax and Bolinas, is not an ordinary engineering feat.

The 34-foot increase in height necessitates the construction of virtually a new dam, 110 feet high on the downstream side of the original dam, and this concrete block is separated by a 3-foot gap between the old and new dams.

The concrete blocks are water cooled at present, but a huge refrigeration plant is being constructed below the dam which will circulate ice water to quickly cool the last pour of grout which will be made in the 3-foot space between the old and new concrete. The reason for this, according to General Manager J. S. Peters, is to bring the temperature of the two concrete blocks to approximately the same degree, otherwise the new concrete, when it finally cools off, would shrink from one to two inches, thus causing ruptures or cracks in what the engineers are striving for, namely a monolithic block. Following this, the 34 foot increase is poured directly on top of the new foundation which has been fused with the old dam.

The Alpine Dam is the second dam in the world of its type to be raised in such a manner, the Hetch Hetchy Dam being the first; while the Assuan Dam on the River Nile in Egypt has been raised by partial employment of the present methods.

Sausalito News, 24 July 1941

That year the dam claimed another casualty:

Fairfax Man Killed in Fall from Alpine Dam

The raising of Alpine dam, so that Marin may have water for many years, yesterday claimed the life of Carl Schick, Fairfax. The 28-year-old man was killed instantly when he fell while climbing a steel ladder. He struck head first on a cement walk. He was climbing to a higher level to eat his lunch there. He died instantly. He leaves a wife and one child.

Sausalito News, 2 October 1941

The dam was completed in November 1941. Two weeks later the United States entered World War II. Alpine Dam was deemed a possible target of sabotage and army units were permanently stationed there. The Bolinas-Fairfax Road was closed to civilians. In April 1942, a fire at the District's engineering office at the dam resulted in the loss of the engineering drawings and correspondence from the project.

It wasn't until five years later—and nine months after the end of the war—that the road was finally reopened:

War-Closed Route to Tamalpais Open

Newly open to motor travel, after being closed throughout the war is the Marin county road from Fairfax via Alpine reservoir to Bolinas, reports the California State Automobile Association. The road connects with Ridgecrest Boulevard and provides a route from the north to Mt. Tamalpais. The road to the Mountain Theater and the top of Tamalpais is no longer a toll road.

Sausalito News, 16 May 1946

Spillway at Alpine Dam.
Courtesy of MMWD.

Bon Tempe Dam

The following year, the District announced plans for yet another new reservoir. It was similar to the old Tamalpais Dam that was never built, but because of the presence now of Alpine Lake, the dam was proposed to be a third of a mile higher up Lagunitas Creek so it would flood a smaller area than that dam:

Water District Plans New Billion Gallon Reservoir Addition

Potential increase in water storage in Marin County by some billion gallons was disclosed last week when Marin Municipal Water District surveyors commenced preliminary work designed to create a new reservoir and storage area to be known as "Bon Tempe".

The new dam is planned for the lower end of a meadow lying between Alpine and Lagunitas Lakes. Specifications call for a structure 300 feet wide at the base and fanning to 900 at the crest and 60 to 70 feet in height.

Because of its location, with Alpine Dam below to catch any water leakage or a dam failure might let loose, General Manager James S. Peters is hopeful of obtaining ready approval from the state.

Sausalito News, 3 July 1947

Bon Tempe Dam, 98 feet tall and impounding 1.4 billion gallons, was completed in 1949. Bon Tempe Road leading to the base of the dam makes use of the grade of the original 1878 San Rafael-Bolinas Road.

The Bolinas-Fairfax Road and the dams and reservoirs today.

The Bolinas-Fairfax Today

Sometime after the war the Bolinas-Fairfax was paved and it is now a smooth two-lane blacktop road. But it's still a challenge to drive, and even more to maintain. Landslides occur nearly every winter. It was closed to vehicles for much of 2016 due to a major landslide near Alpine Dam. The repairs were completed, but only a month later, the heavy winter rains created more slides and closed it again.

The road no longer serves as a major transportation artery to Bolinas. The town is again isolated, as it was in the 1860s, but now the residents like it that way. They tore down the highway signs directing tourists to the town. There is no industry and little business. They get in and out on good, if winding, roads from Sausalito or Olema. No one really needs the Bolinas-Fairfax any more, but it has great sentimental value to many.

The old road is now used mainly by residents of central Marin to go up to Mount Tamalpais via Ridgecrest Boulevard. It also serves as access to the many trailheads into MMWD's watershed. It remains dear to the hearts of bicyclists, motorcyclists, and those who like to drive winding mountain roads and see spectacular scenery.

Few of today's users know of its long history, its many changes, or its importance in the history of Marin County. Yet traces of the old road remain. In this final chapter, I will show how you can explore some of these former routes.

Start where the road began, at the intersection of CA-1 and the Bolinas-Fairfax. The mileposts show distances from Fairfax, so this is actually milepost 14.65. This is where Jesse Colwell and James Wilkins started construction in June of 1878. The ranch of W. W. Wilkins and his self-closing gate is on your left. The farmhouse still stands.

The initial portion is a causeway across a small wetland. At mile 14.37 the road starts its unbroken climb to Bolinas Ridge.

The beginning of the Bolinas-Fairfax Road. CA-1, the Shoreline Highway, in the foreground. Olema is to the left, Sausalito to the right, Bolinas behind you.

Follow the Bolinas-Fairfax up the grade. You are ascending Pike County Gulch. This is where the great fire occurred in 1890, when all the canyons on this side of the ridge burned in less than half an hour, all the way down to Stinson Beach. Trapped by the flames with a fully-loaded stagecoach, driver Leonard Nott left the road, tied his wheels to keep them from turning, and skidded down one of these steep slopes all the way to Bolinas. Look down into the canyon and ponder that.

Just after a major switchback to the right (notice the watering trough for the horses on your left), the road crosses Pike County

Water trough on Bolinas Grade.

Creek and crosses into another canyon, at that time called Thompson Gulch, now Garden Club Canyon. At mile 11.43, you cross that creek and continue traversing the slope into a third canyon. At 10.94 you cross the head of Picher Canyon, originally called Bourne Canyon. So far, this section is essentially just as laid out by Hiram Austin in 1878.

At the top of the ridge, 1500 feet above the ocean, the views will leave you breathless, especially if you arrived by bike or on foot. At mile 10.3 Ridgecrest Road turns off to your right and continues to Rock Spring and on to the three peaks of Tamalpais. This road also has not changed since it was built in 1925. A toll booth once stood just to the south to collect tolls for the Tamalpais Ridgecrest Boulevard Company. Just beyond is the orchard abandoned by the Longleys in 1892.

Bolinas Laoon in the foreground, Bolinas on its point beyond.

On your left in the redwood grove just north of the intersection is the site of Larsen's Summit House. The stagecoach pulled in under a large rustic sign over the entrance, with cut branches spelling out the word

Site of Larsen's Summit House.

187

"Larsen's." This is where the Greek master chef Constantine de Sella served his famous meals—and where he was driven out when fire swept across the ridge in 1904. The fire started at the Hasbrouk place just north of the Summit House. Only a few bricks and melted bottles mark the site now.

The grade down the east slope has been changed near the top, where there used to be more and shorter switchbacks, but below that it is unchanged. There are a number of unbelievably sharp hairpin turns. At mile 9.80 you will pass another watering trough on your right.

Mailbox Curve. Photo by Brad Rippe.

The sharp hairpin turn at mile 9.71 is Mailbox Curve, where the Longleys up on Ridgecrest came to get their mail from the hollow redwood that still stands inside the curve. The old trail to their place starts on the outside of the curve, but soon fades away.

Near the bottom of the grade at mile 8.33, at the Cataract Trailhead, park for a short walk. Follow the Cataract Trail down toward the water. When it starts up toward Laurel Dell, the old stage road can still be seen on the left, descending into Alpine Lake. The old road crossed Cataract Creek on a bridge in the bottom of this gulch—the track can still be discerned when the lake is very low. It then turned downstream, now under the lake. Return to your car.

Cataract Trailhead.

Just below Cataract, you cross the sweep of Alpine Dam at mile 7.80. It's worth stopping here to get out and examine the view, especially if the water is flowing over the spillway and pouring down the huge concrete steps. If it is, go down the fire road on the far side. Stroll down through the ancient redwoods and the roar of falling water to the riverside and double back upstream toward the dam. An old rock dam lies in the creek below you, perhaps associated with Shaver's sawmill.

Alpine Dam in full spate.

Standing on the dam, you are 150 feet above the site of Isaac Shaver's sawmill. The short-lived settlement (1865 to 1873) of millers' and loggers' houses clustered around Cataract Canyon and on the downstream side of the dam. A hundred yards or so upstream, the old road crossed Lagunitas Bridge to the west bank, then turned right and followed Lagunitas Creek upstream. On the right, Frederick Peters had his cabin on the banks of the creek, with his suspension bridges and swimming bowers. Here the two Berkeley co-eds were arrested for wading in 1923.

189

Continue across the dam and make the sharp right along the lake. This first short section was built in 1941 when Alpine Dam was raised and the approaches had to be changed. When originally built in 1916, it was 38 feet lower. It is strange to think that the old dam is still inside the current dam, on the upstream side.

Looking up Alpine Lake just above the dam. Oat Hill behind.

After the first turn, you are on the road built in 1917 by A. J. Fairbanks to move the road up from the valley below when the original dam was built. At mile 7.45, pause to look across the lake. The canyon on the far side is Swede George Gulch, where a deaf-mute logger once had his solitary cabin. Just to the left of the gulch is where Kent's cabin and numerous others once lined the banks of the creek. The Kent Trail still ascends the mountain from the site.

The road traverses around several more gulches and spurs. At milepost 5.88 it makes a deep dip into a large canyon. This is Lily Gulch, with Lily Lake below on the right. The lake was formed in a colossal landslide four centuries ago. Once larger and a popular fishing spot, it was silting in until dredged by the Water District in 1988. The Lily Gulch trail ascends the canyon to the Oat Hill Road, past the impressive Dutchman's Rock (no, I don't know which Dutchman). At mile 5.22 is another trough for the stage horses. The water is no longer potable, though the tadpoles seem to like it.

190

Bolinas-Fairfax Road near Liberty Ranch.

At mile 4.37, the road enters another major canyon. This is Liberty Gulch, formerly Curtis Gulch. The old ranch stood under the lake near where Liberty Gulch meets the main body of Alpine Lake. The foundations built by Vincent and Mary Jane Liberty in the 1860s are still there under the water, but only visible during droughts. Across the lake to the northeast, an old road can just be made out slanting up to the left. This is the Liberty Gulch Road, the bypass of the Bolinas-Fairfax built in 1910 to avoid the reservoir of the never-built Tamalpais Dam.

Where the road crosses Liberty Creek at milepost 4.83, the Old Sled Trail climbs the canyon on the left and on to Little Carson Falls, a favorite hiking destination. This trail was used by the Libertys to bring the milk down to the dairy on wooden sledges from the pastures above Little Carson Falls.

Soon after this switchback, the road emerges from the forest and starts climbing a steep chaparral-covered hillside. Partway up this grade at milepost 4.16, a trail on the right is the old 1910 bypass, known as the Old Liberty Gulch Road. Park here for a short excursion on foot along this long-unused road to Alpine Lake.

The road disappears and turns into a rough trail, overgrown with invasive broom. Just beyond is a deep trench cut into the hillside. A similar trench can be made out on the far side of the lake. These are the excavations for the Tamalpais Dam. It was planned to be higher than Bon Tempe Dam, visible straight ahead.

Returning to the Bolinas-Fairfax, you climb to a saddle at milepost 3.75. On the right is Azalea Hill, offering an easy walk to spectacular panoramas of Mount Tamalpais rising behind Alpine and Bon Tempe Lakes. On the left, Pine Mountain Fire Road winds up a long ridge and leads to scores of trails,

Foundations of Tamalpais Dam, normally under Alpine Lake. Photo by Brad Rippe.

including Little Carson Falls and Pine Mountain, at 1,762 feet the second-highest point in Marin. The Pine Mountain Tunnel, built in 1916 to carry the water from Alpine Dam to San Rafael, runs more than nine hundred feet below this ridge.

Looking down Lagunitas Valley from Azalea Hill. The road in Liberty Gulch is visible below. Beyond Alpine Lake is Bolinas Ridge.

After crossing the saddle, the road curves left above a high steep drop-off on the right. Soon the Meadow Club Golf Course appears in the shallow valley on the right. This area would have been flooded by

192

the Tamalpais Dam. Across the road to the left, the east end of the Pine Mountain Tunnel emerges in the canyon far below.

At mile 1.40, Sky Oaks Road enters from the right. This is the site of the Jory Gate, the entrance to William and Lucy Jory's ranch. The road you just came down is the bypass to Liberty ranch to avoid Alpine Lake. Hiram Austin's 1884 Fairfax Grade came up to this point from the Fairfax railroad station, where the Fairfax Parkade is now, then went up the present Sky Oaks Road. To follow the old road to San Rafael, turn right here.

The road climbs steeply. On the left is the steep dropoff where a painter's wagon frightened the stagecoach team in 1892 and the stage somersaulted down the bank with driver Thad Lewis, two horses, and nine passengers. It is hard to believe no one was seriously injured.

Pass Sky Oaks Ranger Station to the new ticket kiosk on the right (there's a day use fee). Continue to the junction with Bon Tempe Road and turn right to the parking lot. This is the old San Rafael-Bolinas Road. Continue on foot toward Alpine Lake until you reach Bullfrog Road. In 1898, there was a bridge across the creek here called Cattle Bridge. This is where Victor Colwell held up Wallace Sayers' stagecoach on September 19, 1898. Across the creek and a bit to the south is the excavation for Tamalpais Dam that you visited on your previous hike. If Alpine Lake is full, it isn't possible to cross Bon Tempe Creek at this point, so return to your car.

The site of Bontempi Ranch is under the north end of Bon Tempe Dam on your right. Swiss brothers Joseph and Pasqual Bautumpi leased the Lagunitas Dairy Tract and produced milk and butter here.

Drive back up Bon Tempe Road to the intersection with Sky Oaks Road. The original road turned right here; the 1884 Fairfax Grade split off to the north to go to Fairfax. Turn right on Sky Oaks Road for just a few hundred yards to where a dirt road turns off to the left. This is Shaver Grade, which is the original road to San Rafael. Here you will have to leave the car and continue on foot. Have someone meet you at Natalie Coffin Greene Park in Ross.

In about a quarter mile, a faint unmarked trail goes off to the right. Now called the Old Logging Trail, this was the Old Shaver Grade, where Isaac Shaver hauled his lumber to his docks at Ross Landing. It was abandoned when the new Shaver Grade was built in 1878, but was still used occasionally when the new road washed out.

193

Old Shaver Grade.

Continuing on Shaver Grade, the road climbs over a saddle and descends to a major junction called Five Corners (six, actually). The road to the left is Concrete Pipe Road, leading back across the Bolinas-Fairfax to the eastern portal of the Pine Mountain Tunnel. This road and the pipeline beneath were built in 1916 to bring water from Alpine Lake to Ross and San Rafael. Turn sharp right to remain on both Shaver Grade and Concrete Pipe.

This grade, though not as steep as the Old Shaver or Fish Grades to the south, must have been a challenge for the stagecoach teams. At the fork, keep left to stay on Shaver Grade. Partway down the grade, Hidden Meadow Trail turns off to the left. The Porteous family ran the Hippolyte Dairy in the meadow across the creek—only an old stone wall remains now.

Continue another half mile to Phoenix Junction. On your right, the Fish Gulch Trail climbs steeply to Bon Tempe Lake. On the other side of the gulch, Fish Grade Road was built in the 1940s to give easier access to the lake. Straight ahead, John Oscar Eldridge's 1884 Eldridge Grade starts its long 5.8-mile climb to Tamalpais. You may wish to save that climb for another day. Instead, turn left along the north shore of Phoenix Lake. Here you leave the old road, as it ran along the banks of Phoenix Creek and was submerged when the Phoenix Dam was built in 1908.

In six-tenths of a mile you pass a redwood log cabin on the left. This was the 1893 home of Martin Grant, the foreman for the Porteous Ranch. Now owned by MMWD, efforts are being made to restore and preserve it.

Porteous log cabin. Photo courtesy of Preservation Architecture, 2014.

At the dam, look right toward Tamalpais. The canyon across the lake is Bill Williams Gulch, where the old Marin Water Company had a small dam, still visible with a bit of a climb.

Passing Phoenix Dam, you descend into Natalie Coffin Greene Park. Take the trail on the right down into the picnic grounds. The dirt road there is the original road emerging from under the dam. The bridge is the site of Austin's Bridge #1, which was later repaired with a rope. Beyond the parking lot, it turns into Lagunitas Road and enters the town of Ross.

On your right you'll pass the Lagunitas Country Club, which contains part of the structure of Joseph Escallier's notorious Pink Saloon, where hunters and loggers drank, and his partner Mrs. Smith's establishment next door, where they took further entertainment.

Pause at the intersection of Sylvan Lane. The 1874 North Pacific Coast Railroad crossed here on its way between Sausalito and San Anselmo. The railway station was on the right (now the Ross Post Office). Continue to the intersection of Sir Francis Drake Boulevard. This was formerly the Ross Landing Road. To the left was Junction, later San Anselmo. Less than a mile to the right was Ross Landing (now the site of the College of Marin), with docks for loading and unloading schooners and steamers that came up Corte Madera Creek. Isaac Shaver owned one of the docks for the lumber he was bringing out.

To continue following the original stagecoach road, turn left on Drake and an immediate right onto Laurel Grove. Follow it to Makin Grade Road. This is the beginning of the road built by Robert Makin in 1878 to connect Ross to San Rafael. At the top of the ridge, Upper Toyon joins from the right. Turn left to remain on Makin Grade Road. In 200 feet Makin Grade Road descends to the right, but the stage road turned left here onto what it now Upper Toyon.

Descending Brewery Grade.

In another 200 feet, a dirt road descends on the right, crossing into San Rafael. This is the old stage line, nearly as Robert Makin built it. Near the bottom it circles around a ravine. This is the site of the San Rafael Brewery, which brewed lager for almost fifty years, from 1871 to 1918. For this reason

Stagecoach Road monument.

the grade on the north side of the ridge was known as Brewery Grade.

Slated for development, this grade was purchased in January 2017 by neighbors Tamra Peters and William Carney, who donated it to the city of San Rafael, preserving one of the few remaining original sections of the 1879 road. A plaque commemorates this generous gift.

The stagecoach road emerges at the end of Greenwood Avenue. Follow Greenwood to Clark Street and turn left. Turn right onto Ross

Avenue. On your left at 112 Ross Avenue is, oddly enough, the oldest surviving house in San Anselmo. It was built in 1865 by the first settler in San Anselmo, Mexican soldier Domingo Sais (the site is now 57 Sais Avenue). The old family home was moved here to San Rafael in 1892.

Turn left on D Street, then right onto Fourth (if you're traveling by car, you'll have to go around a block to avoid the one-way street). When you reach A Street you can see on your left the site of the 1817 mission that created San Rafael. On the hill above it is the spring that supplied the mission and the Miwok town of Awani-wi before that. The water from this spring still flows down through Boyd Park.

At this intersection, on June 28, 1846, during the Bear Flag Revolt, explorer Kit Carson gunned down three unarmed Mexican gentlemen, 61-year-old José de los Reyes Berreyessa and 19-year-old twins Ramon and Francisco de Haro. The orders were given by Major Charles Frémont, and it later cost him the 1864 presidential election.

On the northwest corner is the site of Hiram Austin's survey office.

Continuing down the block, the square on the left is the site of the first Marin County Courthouse, built in 1872. It burned down in 1971, the result of arson. In the basement was the jail where the young highwayman Victor Colwell was kept in the haunted cell in 1898. Across the street on the right is the site of the Marin Stables, where the stagecoach lines kept their horses and coaches.

Continue east to Tamalpais Avenue and turn right. On your left is the site of the railroad station (recently converted back into a station for the SMART train). This is where passengers from Bolinas would have disembarked from the stage.

And so we complete the route of the old stagecoach line across Marin, nearly from coast to coast. This is the route surveyed by Hiram Austin, built by Jesse Colwell, and driven by those "masters of the ribbons" Henry Gibson, Bob Cottingham, Leonard Nott, and Al Sayers.

The stagecoaches and the men who drove them are gone, but the Bolinas-Fairfax remains, a source of pride and pleasure for the residents of Marin.

Index

201

202

Other Books on Local History by
Brian K. Crawford
Available from Amazon

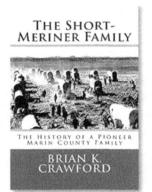

The Short-Meriner Family
60 pages, with 8 maps and 12 illustrations. $8.

A fictionalized account of the arrival in Marin County of the Short-Meriner family in 1846. The family became prominent Marin pioneers and once owned much of San Rafael and San Anselmo (including my own home). Jane Meriner, a 37-year-old widow, her two teenage sons by her first marriage, J. O. B. and Jacob Short, and her small daughters by her second husband, Elizabeth and Catherine Meriner, drove their covered wagon along the California Trail from Missouri to San Rafael. They were friends of the Donner party and traveled part of the way with them, crossing Roller Pass instead of Donner Pass and getting across just before the storm that doomed the Donners. Since there are many accounts of the California Trail, this account describes only the final part of their journey, from the end of the Trail at Johnson's Rancho in Yolo County and across the Central Valley to the San Rafael Mission, where they lived in the abandoned buildings.

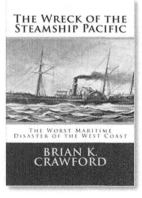

The Wreck of the Steamship *Pacific*
73 pages, with one map and 17 illustrations. $7.

On the evening of Thursday, November 4, 1875, the steamship *Pacific* collided with the clipper ship *Orpheus* off Cape Flattery in Washington. The *Orpheus* resumed her journey but went aground the following day and was lost. The *Pacific* – old, unsafe, and dangerously overcrowded – broke up in minutes and went down, scattering hundreds of men, women, and children into the sea. Exactly how many died will never be known, but the names we know are enough to make this the worst maritime disaster in the history of the West Coast. Only two men survived, and their first-hand accounts are here. The passengers included many wealthy and famous people, along with gold miners, singers, actors, and an equestrian troupe. One passenger had already survived three other shipwrecks on the same passage. Several were carrying large amounts of gold. The stories of how they came to be aboard that night are as interesting as the disaster itself. In period newspaper articles, letters, diaries, and mysterious notes in bottles, the tales are told.

The Captains – Jefferson Davis Howell (brother-in-law of President Jefferson Davis) of the *Pacific*, and Charles Sawyer of the *Orpheus* – were both young but very experienced. Who was at fault? Were they drunk? Could the collision have been averted, or more lives saved? Were the ships safe? Were the officers and crews and owners competent? Was there an official cover-up? Was the "last will in a bottle" genuine? We will examine the evidence.

Illustrated with photographs and drawings of the ships and participants, this volume examines all aspects of a singular disaster. The poignancy of the deaths, and the devastation felt by so many left behind, made a mark on a generation that they remembered the rest of their lives. In the impact it had on people's lives and imaginations, the sinking of the *Pacific* was the *Titanic* of its era.

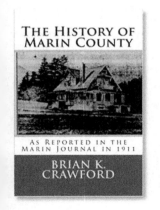

THE HISTORY OF MARIN COUNTY

AS REPORTED IN THE MARIN JOURNAL IN 1911

BRIAN K. CRAWFORD

The History of Marin County
79 pages, with 34 illustrations. $7.50.

In 1911, the *Marin Journal*, forerunner of the *Marin Independent Journal*, published a special Golden Anniversary edition commemorating its first fifty years of publication. Sixteen pages long and printed on book-quality paper, the edition consisted entirely of a series of illustrated articles about each community in Marin County, each written by a local correspondent, extolling the virtues of their towns. These give an intriguing view of how local residents viewed their communities, their progress, and their hopes for the future, more than a century ago. The pride and their hopes glow through their words.

The special edition was followed by a series of weekly articles detailing the history of Marin County. While there are many inaccuracies, these articles were written when many of the founding pioneers of the county were still alive, and contain much information not available elsewhere. While there are many histories of California, this series focuses on Marin County alone and describes the people and events that made the county and formed its culture. Taken together, the special edition and the history articles give an intimate look at the county as seen by its founders and residents more than a century ago.

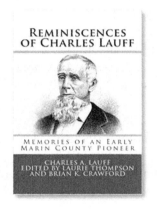

Reminiscences of Charles Lauff

73 pages, with a portrait of Lauff, a map of the Mexican land grants in Marin County, and extensively annotated. $10.

In 1916, at age 94, Charles August Lauff (1822- 1917) narrated the reminiscences that follow in a series of articles for the San Rafael Independent. The picture he paints of Marin County provides us with a glimpse of the County's early topography and settlers, bringing to life the rancho era and the personalities of such original land grantees as Timothy Murphy, John Reed and William Richardson. In addition, he recounts his experiences during the Gold Rush and provides details about life in San Francisco, Sacramento and other burgeoning towns in Northern California.

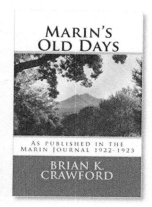

Marin's Old Days

203 pages, extensively annotated. $14.

In 1922-1923, the *Marin Journal*, forerunner of the *Marin Independent Journal*, published a series of fifty-eight articles called Marin's Old Days, recounting the history of Marin County up to that time. While in some cases inaccurate by current knowledge, these articles reveal interesting history, fascinating pioneer characters, and the way Marin residents viewed their county nearly 100 years ago.

Made in the USA
Middletown, DE
25 March 2023

27670291R00119